DATE DUE

Creation of the Modern Middle East

Oman

Creation of the Modern Middle East

Oman

Calvin H. Allen, Jr.

Introduction by
Akbar Ahmed
School of International Service
American University

CHELSEA HOUSE
P U B L I S H E R S
A Haights Cross Communications Company
Philadelphia

Frontispiece: Fort Jalali, 1905
The 16th-century Portuguese fort still dominates Muscat's harbor.

CHELSEA HOUSE PUBLISHERS

EDITOR IN CHIEF Sally Cheney
DIRECTOR OF PRODUCTION Kim Shinners
CREATIVE MANAGER Takeshi Takahashi
MANUFACTURING MANAGER Diann Grasse

Staff for OMAN

EDITOR Lee Marcott
PRODUCTION ASSISTANT Jaimie Winkler
PICTURE RESEARCHER Sarah Bloom
SERIES DESIGNER Keith Trego
COVER DESIGNER Keith Trego
LAYOUT 21st Century Publishing and Communications, Inc.

A Haights Cross Communications Company

http://www.chelseahouse.com

3 5 7 9 8 6 4 2

Library of Congress Cataloging-in-Publication Data

Allen, Calvin H.
   Oman / Calvin H. Allen, Jr.
      p. cm.—(Creation of the modern Middle East)
Includes bibliographical references and index.
   ISBN 0-7910-6508-1
   1. Oman—History—20th century. [1. Oman—History—20th century.]
I. Title. II. Series.
DS247.O68 A585 2002
953.5305—dc21
                                                        2002006889

Table of Contents

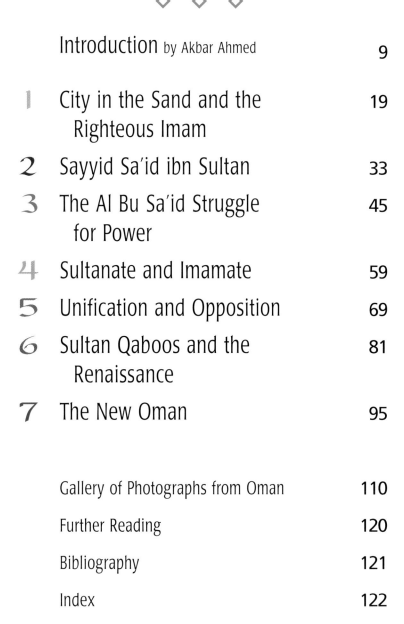

Index to the Photographs

Creation of the Modern Middle East

Iran

Iraq

Israel

Jordan

The Kurds

Kuwait

Oman

Palestinian Authority

Saudi Arabia

Syria

Turkey

Yemen

Introduction

Akbar Ahmed

The Middle East, it seems, is always in the news. Unfortunately, most of the news is of a troubling kind. Stories of suicide bombers, hijackers, street demonstrations, and ongoing violent conflict dominate these reports. The conflict draws in people living in lands far from the Middle East; some support one group, some support another, often on the basis of kinship or affinity and not on the merits of the case.

The Middle East is often identified with the Arabs. The region is seen as peopled by Arabs speaking Arabic and belonging to the Islamic faith. The stereotype of the Arab oil sheikh is a part of contemporary culture. But both of these images—that the Middle East is in perpetual anarchy and that it has an exclusive Arab identity—are oversimplifications of the region's complex contemporary reality.

In reality, the Middle East is an area that straddles Africa and Asia and has a combined population of over 200 million people inhabiting over twenty countries. It is a region that draws the entire world into its politics and, above all, it is the land that is the birth place of the three great Abrahamic faiths—Judaism, Christianity, and Islam. The city of Jerusalem is the point at which these three faiths come together and also where they tragically confront one another.

It is for these reasons that knowledge of the Middle East will remain of importance and that news from it will remain ongoing and interesting.

Let us consider the stereotype of the Middle East as a land of constant anarchy. It is easy to forget that some of the greatest lawgivers and people of peace were born, lived, and died here. In the Abrahamic tradition these names are a glorious roll call of human history—Abraham, Moses, Jesus, and Muhammad. In the tradition of the Middle East, where these names are especially revered, people often add the blessing "Peace be upon him" when speaking their names.

The land is clearly one that is shared by the great faiths. While it has a dominant Muslim character because of the large Muslim population, its Jewish and Christian presence must not be underestimated. Indeed, it is the dynamics of the relationships between the three faiths that allow us to enter the Middle East today and appreciate the points where these faiths come together or are in conflict.

To understand the predicament in which the people of the Middle East find themselves today, it is well to keep the facts of history before us. History is never far from the minds of the people in this region. Memories of the first great Arab dynasty, the Umayyads (661-750), based in Damascus, and the even greater one of the Abbasids (750-1258), based in Baghdad, are still kept alive in books and folklore. For the Arabs, their history, their culture, their tradition, their language, and above all their religion, provide them with a rich source of pride; but the glory of the past contrasts with the reality and powerlessness of contemporary life.

Many Arabs have blamed past rulers for their current situation beginning with the Ottomans who ruled them until World War I and then the European powers that divided their lands. When they achieved independence after World War II they discovered that the artificial boundaries created by the European powers cut across tribes and clans. Today, too, they complain that a form of Western imperialism still dominates their politics and rulers.

Again, while it is true that Arab history and Arab temperament have colored the Middle East strongly, there are other distinct peoples who have made a significant contribution to the culture of the region. Turkey is one such non-Arab nation with its own language, culture, and contribution to the region through the influence of the Ottoman Empire. Memories of that period for the Arabs are mixed, but what cannot be denied are the spectacular administrative and architectural achievements of the Ottomans. It is the longest dynasty in world history, beginning in 1300 and ending after World War I in 1922, when Kemal Ataturk wished to reject the past on the way to creating a modern Turkey.

Similarly, Iran is another non-Arab country with its own rich language and culture. Based in the minority sect of Islam, the Shia, Iran has often been in opposition to its Sunni neighbors, both Arab and Turk. Perhaps this confrontation helped to forge a unique Iranian, or Persian, cultural identity that, in turn, created the brilliant art, architecture, and poetry under the Safawids (1501-1722). The Safawid period also saw the establishment of the principle of interference or participation—depending on one's perspective—in matters of the state by the religious clerics. So while the Ayatollah Khomeini was very much a late 20th century figure, he was nonetheless reflecting the patterns of Iranian history.

Israel, too, represents an ancient, non-Arabic, cultural and religious tradition. Indeed, its very name is linked to the tribes that figure prominently in the stories of the Bible and it is through Jewish tradition that memory of the great biblical patriarchs like Abraham and Moses is kept alive. History is not a matter of years, but of millennia, in the Middle East.

Perhaps nothing has evoked as much emotional and political controversy among the Arabs as the creation of the state of Israel in 1948. With it came ideas of democracy and modern culture that seemed alien to many Arabs. Many saw the wars that followed stir further conflict and hatred; they also saw the wars as an inevitable clash between Islam and Judaism.

It is therefore important to make a comment on Islam and Judaism. The roots of prejudice against Jews can be anti-Semitic, anti-Judaic, and anti-Zionist. The prejudice may combine all three and there is often a degree of overlap. But in the case of the Arabs, the matter is more complicated because, by definition, Arabs cannot be anti-Semitic because they themselves are considered Semites. They cannot be anti-Judaic, because Islam recognizes the Jews as "people of the Book."

What this leaves us with is the clash between the political philosophy of Zionism, which is the establishment of a Jewish nation in Palestine, and Arab thought. The antagonism of the Arabs to Israel may result in the blurring of lines. A way must be found by Arabs and Israelis to live side by side in peace. Perhaps recognition of the common Abrahamic tradition is one way forward.

The hostility to Israel partly explains the negative coverage the Arabs get in the Western media. Arab Muslims are often accused of being anarchic and barbaric due to the violence of the Middle East. Yet, their history has produced some of the greatest figures in history.

Consider the example of Sultan Salahuddin Ayyoubi, popularly called Saladin in Western literature. Saladin had vowed to take revenge for the bloody massacres that the Crusaders had indulged in when they took Jerusalem in 1099. According to a European eyewitness account the blood in the streets was so deep that it came up to the knees of the horsemen.

Yet, when Saladin took Jerusalem in 1187, he showed the essential compassion and tolerance that is at the heart of the Abrahamic faiths. He not only released the prisoners after ransom, as was the custom, but paid for those who were too poor to afford any ransom. His nobles and commanders were furious that he had not taken a bloody revenge. Saladin is still remembered in the bazaars and villages as a leader of great learning and compassion. When contemporary leaders are compared to Saladin, they are usually found wanting. One reason may be that the problems of the region are daunting.

The Middle East faces three major problems that will need solutions in the twenty-first century. These problems affect society and politics and need to be tackled by the rulers in those lands and all other people interested in creating a degree of dialogue and participation.

The first of the problems is that of democracy. Although democracy is practiced in some form in a number of the Arab countries, for the majority of ordinary people there is little sense of participation in their government. The frustration of helplessness in the face of an indifferent bureaucracy at the lower levels of administration is easily converted to violence. The indifference of the state to the pressing needs of the "street" means that other non-governmental organizations can step in. Islamic organizations offering health and education programs to people in the shantytowns and villages have therefore emerged and flourished over the last decades.

The lack of democracy also means that the ruler becomes remote and autocratic over time as he consolidates his power. It is not uncommon for many rulers in the Middle East to pass on their rule to their son. Dynastic rule, whether kingly or based in a dictatorship, excludes ordinary people from a sense of participation in their own governance. They need to feel empowered. Muslims need to feel that they are able to participate in the process of government. They must feel that they are able to elect their leaders into office and if these leaders do not deliver on their promises, that they can throw them out. Too many of the rulers are nasty and brutish. Too many Muslim leaders are kings and military dictators. Many of them ensure that their sons or relatives stay on to perpetuate their dynastic rule.

With democracy, Muslim peoples will be able to better bridge the gaps that are widening between the rich and the poor. The sight of palatial mansions with security guards carrying automatic weapons standing outside them and, alongside, hovels teeming with starkly poor children is a common one in Muslim cities. The distribution of wealth must remain a priority of any democratic government.

The second problem in the Middle East that has wide ramifications in society is that of education. Although Islam emphasizes knowledge and learning, the sad reality is that the standards of education are unsatisfactory. In addition, the climate for scholarship and intellectual activity is discouraging. Scholars are too often silenced, jailed, or chased out of the country by the administration. The sycophants and the intelligence services whose only aim is to tell the ruler what he would like to hear, fill the vacuum.

Education needs to be vigorously reformed. The *madrassah,* or religious school, which is the institution that provides primary education for millions of boys in the Middle East, needs to be brought into line with the more prestigious Westernized schools reserved for the elite of the land. By allowing two distinct streams of education to develop, Muslim nations are encouraging the growth of two separate societies: a largely illiterate and frustrated population that is susceptible to leaders with simple answers to the world's problems and a small, Westernized, often corrupt and usually uncaring group of elite. The third problem facing the Middle East is that of representation in the mass media. Although this point is hard to pin down, the images in the media are creating problems of understanding and communication in the communities living in the Middle East. Muslims, for example, will always complain that they are depicted in negative stereotypes in the non-Arab media. The result of the media onslaught that plagues Muslims is the sense of anger on the one hand and the feeling of loss of dignity on the other. Few Muslims will discuss the media rationally. Greater Muslim participation in the media and greater interaction will help to solve the problem. But it is not so simple. The Israelis also complain of the stereotypes in the Arab media that depict them negatively.

Muslims are aware that their religious culture represents a civilization rich in compassion and tolerance. They are aware that given a period of stability in which they can grapple with the problems of democracy, education, and self-image they can take their rightful place in the community of nations. However painful the current reality, they do carry an idea of an ideal human society with them. Whether a Turk, or an Iranian, or an Arab, every Muslim is aware of the message that the prophet of Islam brought to this region in the seventh century. This message still has resonance for these societies. Here are words from the last address of the prophet spoken to his people:

> All of you descend from Adam and Adam was made of earth. There is no superiority for an Arab over a non-Arab nor for a non-Arab over an Arab, neither for a white man over a black man nor a black man over a white man . . . the noblest among you is the one who is most deeply conscious of God.

This is a noble and worthy message for the twenty-first century in the Middle East. Not only Muslims, but Jews, and Christians would agree with it. Perhaps its essential theme of tolerance, compassion, and equality can help to rediscover the wellsprings of tradition that can both inspire and unite.

It is for these reasons that I congratulate Chelsea House Publishers for taking the initiative in helping us to understand the Middle East through this series. The story of the Middle East is, in many profound ways, the story of human civilization.

— **Dr. Akbar S. Ahmed**
The Ibn Khaldun Chair of Islamic Studies and
Professor of International Relations,
School of International Service
American University

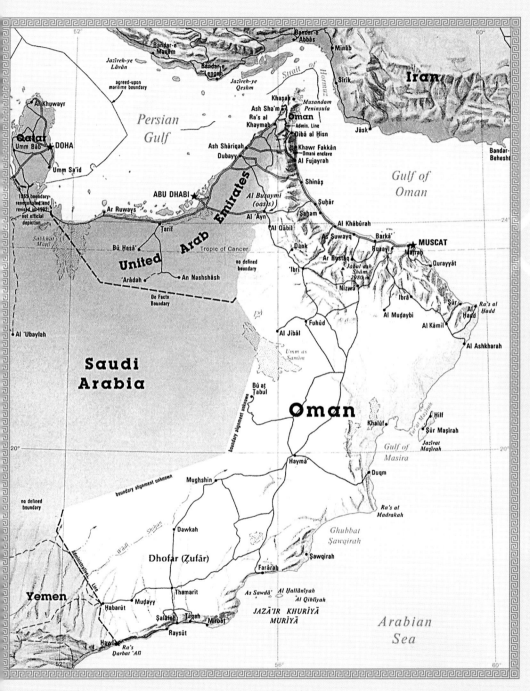

Modern Map of Oman

The Matrah Camel Caravan, 1901

A camel caravan shown about to depart from outside the Matrah city wall. A caravan is a group of merchants or travelers journeying together for protection. In deserts, the camel is the animal most commonly used because of its ability to go without water for several days.

1

City in the Sand and the Righteous Imam

Nicholas Clapp had a dream: Find Ubar, an ancient city that the famous Arabian traveler T. E. Lawrence—perhaps better known as Lawrence of Arabia—had called "the Atlantis of the sands" after the mythical civilization of the Mediterranean destroyed by a massive flood. While Atlantis had disappeared under the waters, the Arab myth of Ubar had this center of the frankincense trade buried in the sands of the Rub al-Khali, the great Empty Quarter of southern Arabia, in Dhofar province of modern Oman.

Clapp was a most unlikely discoverer. He was not an explorer but a filmmaker. His introduction to Oman had come in the 1970s while

19

producing a film on Omani government efforts to preserve the Arabian oryx, a nearly extinct long-horned desert antelope that might be the origins of the legend of the unicorn. While working on that project, he read Bertram Thomas's classic tale of Arabian travel, *Arabia Felix*. Thomas recounted his tale of Ubar, and Clapp was smitten.

Thomas had been the first European to dream of discovering Ubar, but he was not the last. Many famous Arabian travelers had sought this great prize. In 1930 Thomas's Arab guides had pointed out to him the camel tracks that lead to Ubar. He followed the route for a short time before abandoning the quest in favor of becoming the first European to cross the mighty sands. In 1932 Harry St. John Philby, crossing much the same territory as Thomas, devoted a whole chapter in his *The Empty Quarter*, to Wabar (another name for Ubar). But his site was merely a crater field in the heart of desert, much too far inland to have been the mythical city. Wilfred Thesiger makes mention of the buried city of the 'Ad (yet another name for Ubar) and of having seen the caravan tracks in classic *Arabian Sands*, but he had never tried to find the site. Wendell Phillips, an American archaeologist, had twice in the 1950s set out to discover the city, his efforts relying on four-wheel drive vehicles rather than camels. He, too—as described in his book *Unknown Oman*—followed the camel tracks described by Thomas. Despite all of these efforts, no one found the city. The great prize remained unclaimed.

While Thomas, Philby, Thesiger, and Phillips had all relied on local Arab tradition and stories collected while in the sands, Clapp began his search in the comforts of the Huntington Library in San Marino, California, in 1981, seeking out all possible literary references to an ancient city in Dhofar. There Clapp found documentation of an Omanum Emporium on maps produced by the second-century

Alexandrian geographer Claudius Ptolemy, the city of Iram mentioned in the Koran and described in Arab legend as having been buried in the sands for the wickedness that its wealth had brought to it, and other stories about fabled trade centers in the desert contained in the *Arabian Nights*. Arab historians, particularly al-Hamdani of Yemen, provided more detailed information on Ubar, the city of Shaddad ibn 'Ad, who had built it to rival paradise. In the end, though, the literary sources added little to the information collected on the ground by earlier explorers.

Clapp then hit upon a much more modern approach to archeology: technology in the form of high-resolution space imagery. Phillips had actually used an airplane to trace the tracks of the road to Ubar, but the path disappeared into the sands. From space, though, Clapp could obtain images from a much wider area. Furthermore, digital images collected using nonvisible wavelengths such as infrared revealed new features and characteristics previously unobtainable.

Clapp made his first call to the Jet Propulsion Laboratory in Pasadena, California. Clapp convinced the lab's Dr. Ronald Blom that his search for Ubar was not some crazy idea, and Blom and his colleagues arranged for a 1984 *Challenger* shuttle flight to aim its remote-sensing equipment on Dhofar. Much to everyone's surprise, the images showed ancient tracks in the desert, and not just the "road to Ubar" described to Thomas—in fact, there were tracks all over the place. Blom then obtained photographs of the same area from the American Landsat satellite and the French SPOT satellite. These provided even more verification. Photos taken in nonvisible light revealed the differences between the much finer sand particles of a caravan route, ground down by passing camels, and the surrounding rocky surfaces. These were not detectable from either regular photography or surface observation.

Shaharah Girls, 1930

The Shaharah live in the mountains between Oman and Yemen. It is believed that the Shaharah are descended from the People of 'Ad, an ancient tribe— perhaps the oldest of all in the Arabian peninsula.

In antiquity, these people harvested the finest frankincense from the groves high in the mountains of Dhofar. The ancient city of Ubar, the legendary "Atlantis of the Sands" was a Shaharah staging point for caravans carrying frankincense north to Mesopotamia, Egypt, Greece, and Rome.

In addition to the Arabic, the Shaharah speak their own peculiar chirping, singsong language that the explorers Theodore and Mabel Bent called "the language of the birds." In the 1890's, the Bent's were among the very first westerners to travel through the southern Arabian peninsula. In their book *The Land of Frankincense and Myrrh* (1895), the Bents state that more than 5,000 years ago, the Sumerians called a tribe living near the Persian Gulf "Lulubulu," an onomatopoeic word mimicking the song of birds. (Onomatopoeia means the formation of a word, a *cuckoo* or *boom,* by imitation of a sound.)

In 1998 Nicholas Clapp, the documentary filmmaker who has lectured and written about the ancient city of Ubar, described the Shaharah women that he had met as "elegant; their hair done up in fine braids and tinted blue. [They] had the fragrance of frankincense."

What the remote-sensing images revealed was that "the road to Ubar" was part of a network of caravan paths. Most interestingly, the road appeared to be heading not *to* Ubar but *away* from it. Ubar was not farther out in the desert but was, in fact, very near to the site where Thomas, Thesiger, and Philby had all begun their travels: the well at Shisr (Shisur). But Shisr was a well-known site, about the only fresh water available in the region and guarded by an old fort, probably dating to the 16th century—much too modern to be Ubar.

With his Arab legends, literary references, and remote-sensing images in hand, Clapp next made preparations for fieldwork in Dhofar. Critical to the success of the endeavor was access to the site and archaeological expertise. The first came in the person of Ranulph Fiennes, an explorer in his own right and a person with good connections to Sultan Qaboos ibn Sa'id Al-Sa'id, then the ruler of Oman. Fiennes had served in the Omani army during Sultan Qaboos's fight with Marxist rebels in Dhofar during the 1970s (*see* Chapter 6). Archeological expertise came via Dr. Juris Zarins, a specialist in pre-Islamic archeology of the Arabian Peninsula with experience in working in that hostile environment. Fiennes made the arrangements with the Omani government, and Zarins led the field expedition.

Preliminary ground reconnaissance began in 1990, but it was interrupted by the Iraqi invasion of Kuwait. Then in November 1991 Clapp and the rest of what they had termed the TransArabia Expedition set out on their quest for Ubar. Their exploration of one of the caravan routes discovered by remote imagery led them directly to Shisr. Other roads did the same. Though aware that this well-known site was too modern to be Ubar, Clapp and his team began excavations on the day after Christmas. As they dug around the 16th-century fort, they discovered the remains of an earlier structure. Below that, the archaeologists found earlier structures and ancient pottery shards. Shisr was Ubar! Thomas, Thesiger, and Phillips had all stood on the remains of their prize. All had taken water from its well. But only Clapp and his party had thought to look below the ruins and see what lay beneath.

What Zarins's excavations revealed was a rather small, octagonal-shaped "fort" with nine towers. There are no other structures in the vicinity, but plenty of evidence exists for what must have been a tent city surrounding the fort. Pottery remains dated the original settlement to as early as 3000 B.C. with a "golden age" roughly coinciding with the age of the Roman Empire (500 B.C.–500 A.D.). The fort undoubtedly served as an ancient caravansary—an inn where caravans loaded, unloaded, and stored goods for distribution throughout a trading network. Among the artifacts discovered were a 1,500-year-old chess set, glazed bracelets from Yemen, incense burners, and Roman vessels of various sorts.

What had happened to Ubar? The fort was built over the limestone aquifer, or open cavern, that provided the life-giving water. As the water level subsided, so, too, did the limestone, perhaps cataclysmically because the fort sank into a hole. It was then covered with sand—just as the myth stated.

Ubar represents probably the earliest example of what is a major theme in Omani history down to present time: Oman's role as a participant in world commerce. Ubar was what we would call today a "global city"—an urban area with a cosmopolitan population interacting with all other parts of the world. Frankincense brought the world to Ubar and took Omanis to the Mediterranean and other parts of the Middle East. In later centuries other products and commercial activities saw the rise to prominence of Sohar, then Qalhat, and then Muscat. For about 140 years that commercial importance brought foreign domination as from 1507 to 1649 the Portuguese occupied Muscat and the

Frankincense Tree, c. 1920

These proud owners of a large Dhofar frankincense garden are posing in front of their valuable tree.

The Dhofar region of southern Oman is about the only place in the world where the frankincense tree grows. It produces a sap with a sweet fragrance, that is considered as valuable as gold.

In the ancient world, more than 3,000 tons may have been exported annually to consecrate temples, mask the odor of cremations, make cosmetics, and to treat every conceivable illness. The Egyptians used frankincense to preserve the bodies of pharaohs. Pliny the Elder, the first-century Roman scholar, wrote that the Emperor Nero burned more than the annual Dhofar harvest at the funeral of his wife Poppaea (65 A.D.). And, the three gifts at the birth of Christ—gold, myrrh, and frankincense—were considered the most precious offering of Eastern kingdoms.

In 1993 the government of Oman attempted to revive the tradition of perfumemaking. They commissioned a leading Parisian perfumier to create a new fragrance using frankincense and rose water. *Amouage*, with its silver bottle plated with 24-carat gold, is now one of the most costly perfumes in the world. And in 1995 the company created the scent *Ubar,* which reaches a different economic market in duty-free shops worldwide.

other ports. However, whether under Omani or foreign control, fleets of ships largely replaced the camel caravans as Omani merchants set sail for India, China, East Africa, and, by the 19th century, Europe and the United States. In modern times Muscat has remained a global city, and the product that Oman possesses that the rest of the world so desires has become oil.

THE RIGHTEOUS IMAM: NASIR IBN MURSHID AL-YA'ARIBI

In 1624 the notables of Oman gathered together under the legal scholar Khamis ibn Sa'id al-Shakasi and unanimously elected Nasir ibn Murshid al-Ya'aribi to serve as their *imam* (leader). After much contemplation, Nasir ibn Murshid accepted the decision of the council and agreed "to decree what is lawful and prohibit what is unlawful." Nasir ibn Murshid became the ruler of Oman.

The selection of Nasir ibn Murshid as imam serves to demonstrate a second important theme in Omani history: the relationship between religion and state. Oman is an Islamic state, but the majority of Omanis follow a distinctive form of Islam known as Ibadism, which is different from the Sunni and Shi'ite forms familiar to most Americans. The differences among Sunni, Shi'ite, and Ibadi Muslims are more political than religious and relate specifically to how the leader of the community of Muslims is chosen and the function of that leader.

Sunni Muslims historically believed that their leader was the caliph (*khalifah,* or successor). The caliph was selected by a consensus of the leaders of the community from among all the members of the Quraish, Muhammad's tribe. In time the selection was limited to specific families within the Quraish, such as during the Umayyad (621-750) and Abbasid caliphates (750-1258). The function of the caliph was to insure the protection and security of the community and to administer the law of God (the Shari'a). Interestingly enough, the caliph had no authority to legislate or interpret the law; this function was placed in the hands of legal scholars, the ulema'.

Shi'ites differ from Sunnis in both the selection process and function of their leader, the imam. First, the imam must be a direct descendent of the Prophet Muhammad through his daughter, Fatimah, and her husband, Ali. The reigning imam selects his successor. Secondly, the imam is considered to be, like Muhammad, a perfect man. Therefore, the imam becomes a source of the law; unlike the caliph, the imam can legislate. Today these differences are largely theoretical. The Mongols murdered the last caliph when they conquered Baghdad in 1258, although the Ottoman Sultans claimed the title down to 1923. The last imam, the 12th descendent of the Prophet Muhammad, disappeared in the ninth century and has become a messianic figure.

Ibadism, the form of Islam identified with Oman, differs again from both Sunnism and Shi'ism. The movement goes back to the early years of Islam in 761, during a conflict between Ali, the prophet's son-in-law, and Mua'wiyah, the founder of the Umayyad Caliphate. Both claimed the caliphate and agreed to arbitration to resolve the dispute. A group of dissidents known as the Kharijites, or seceders, rejected the whole notion of the lofty position of caliph being subject to the whim of arbitration. They rejected both caliphs' claims.

In time these Kharijites, under Abdullah ibn Ibad (from whence the name Ibadi), developed their own theory of leadership in which the imam (the same term used by the Shi'ites) was to be chosen by a consensus of the leaders of the community (like the Sunnis) but from among all Muslims. The imam need not be from either the tribe or the family of the Prophet Muhammad. The function of the Ibadi imam very closely followed the practice of the Sunnis: the imam had responsibility for security and defense—although Ibadi principles prohibited the imam from maintaining any kind of standing army—and administered the Shari'a. The imam could not legislate.

Omanis began to elect imams in 751 and continued to do so for the next 400 years. But then for the next 500 years tyrants and kings dominated Omani politics. According to the Omani chroniclers, these tyrants caused widespread evil and oppression. Periodically the Ibadi ideal would be restored, and the notables would gather to elect a new imam. But still, tribal divisions and disagreements eroded the authority of these imams.

Omani society was divided among many tribes. Although a sheikh led most tribes, the most influential of Oman's tribes, such as the Bani Riyam, the Hirth, the Bani Bu Ali, and the Bani Ruwaha, selected a *tamimah*, a tribal leader who actually held the power of life and death over his followers. Furthermore, all tribes claimed allegiance to one or the other of two great confederations, the Yemen and Nizar. The successful imam had to use both his righteousness and military prowess to overcome the interests of the tamimahs and the confederations to establish and maintain power.

Nasir ibn Murshid al-Ya'aribi was just such an imam. Despite his election, no fewer then 14 other kings and tyrants claimed authority in Oman, including the Portuguese in Sohar, Muscat, and other coastal towns. Following his election as imam, Nasir ibn Murshid overcame these rivals one by one. Most often the people of towns and villages invited the imam to overthrow their unjust rulers. On several occasions unscrupulous local rulers pretended to accept the rule of the imam, but their treachery was quickly discovered, and they were eliminated. Nasir ibn Murshid's one failure was that he did not expel the Portuguese from Muscat.

Matrah Gate, 1931

Matrah Gate, also constructed in the late 16th century by the Portuguese, was in Matrah, the neighboring bay to Old Muscat and the site of Oman's ancient port.

    The wall had six towers, each similar to the one in this photograph. This tower is called Sur Ruwi and contains a gate within that is thought to have been Matrah's s oldest on the city's northern side.

Under imam Nasir ibn Murshid, so the chroniclers tell us, Islam flourished, and evil was checked. Many stories relate the favor that Allah bestowed upon him, such as the time that a house collapsed on a group of men who were speaking evil of the imam, how an assassin became paralyzed just as he was to strike the sleeping imam, or how not one person in all of Oman died from attack by wild animals

Ruins of Ancient Persian Aqueduct, Nizwa, 1905

Nizwa is located near the foothills of the al-Hajar mountains. For centuries water from the upland slopes has been channeled by aqueducts (*falaj*) to provided irrigation. The largest *falaj*, pictured above, was built by the Persians in the early 17th century. This water supply has made Nizwa an important agriculture center.

Nizwa was the capital of Oman in the 6th and 7th centuries. Today, it is best known for its large fort and silver market (*souq*). The silver *souq* is considered the best place in Oman to purchase a traditional *khunjar* (ceremonial dagger) made locally by Omani craftsmen.

during the imam's lifetime. Imam Nasir ibn Murshid certainly personified the Ibadi ideal.

Imam Nasir ibn Murshid reigned from 1624 to 1649. Following his death, other members of the Ya'aribah obtained election as imam. In time, though, the 'ulema became dissatisfied with a Ya'aribah dynasty holding the imamate. Tribal leaders also began to oppose Ya'aribah rule.

A great civil war ensued in which Khalf ibn Mubarak, the tamimah of the Bani Hina', gathered the Yemeni tribes, and Muhammad ibn Nasir, tamimah of the Bani Ghafir, gathered the Nizari tribes to support rival imams. From this day on the confederations were known by new names: Hinawi and Ghafiri. One imam invited Persian support, further complicating matters.

Then in 1753 the Ghafiri tribes elected one Ahmad ibn Sa'id Al Bu Sa'id, who had expelled the Persian invaders, to be the imam. Ahmad ibn Sa'id eventually received the support of all Omanis and came close to restoring the glory of Imam Nasir ibn Murshid al-Ya'aribi. In the process he established the regime that currently rules Oman. However, when he died in 1783, his son did not obtain universal recognition as imam. Various family members, all utilizing the title *sayyid* (lord), laid claim to parts of the country, and the sheikhs and tamimahs asserted their authority over large areas. Eventually Imam Ahmad ibn Sa'id's grandson, Sayyid Sa'id ibn Sultan, would establish his authority throughout Oman but not as imam. The imamate ideal would remain, however, a powerful force in Omani politics.

Muscat, 1951

The Persians invaded the Oman coast in 1737. They captured Muscat in 1743. An Omani leader, Ahmad ibn Sa'id, who held the fort at Sohar, continued to fight the Persians. He succeeded in driving them from Oman in 1745. Ahmad ibn Sa'id became imam in 1753, establishing the Al Bu Sa'id dynasty which still rules Oman today.

2

Sayyid Sa'id ibn Sultan

The current ruling dynasty in Oman is the Al Bu Sa'id. This family came to power in about 1745 when Ahmad ibn Sa'id Al Bu Sa'id expelled a Persian army invited to Oman by the last Ya'aribah imam. Ahmad gained election to the imamate in 1753. The first 50 years of Al Bu Sa'id rule were, however, marked by rivalries within the family (all of whom bore the honorific title "sayyid"). Despite the political instability, the port of Muscat became a great commercial center. Eventually, Sayyid Sa'id ibn Sultan Al Bu Sa'id established his authority throughout Oman. He did not, though, become an imam. During his lifetime, Oman became one of the great commercial powers of the Western Indian Ocean region, and the sayyid carved out an empire that stretched and textiles from Europe all made their way through Muscat. Sultan sought to require that every ship bound for the Persian Gulf stop at his capital and pay a transit fee. Muscat became an international city, with Europeans, Africans, Indians, and Arabs residing within its confines and trading the products of the world.

Sultan's murder at the hands of Qawasimi pirates threatened the stability of Muscat. Sultan's 13-year-old son, Sayyid Sa'id ibn Sultan, aided by his aunt, the famous Bibi Mawza, daughter of the imam Ahmad ibn Sa'id, seized control of the port. Unfortunately, nearly every other family member, including his uncles the imam Sa'id and Qais ibn Ahmad, sought to take his prize, touching off civil war. Sa'id called upon the assistance of Sayyid Badr ibn Saif, who, with the help of his Saudi Arabian friends, secured control of Muscat. He also secured control of Sa'id.

Sa'id's alliance with Badr and the Saudis further alienated Imam Sa'id ibn Ahmad and Sayyid Qais, and the civil war continued for the next two years. Sa'id, Badr, and the Ghafiri tribes in alliance with Sheikh Muhammad ibn Nasir al-Jabri, with the support of the Saudis, fought against Imam Sa'id, Qais, other members of the royal family, and the Hinawi tribes. Eventually, several of Sa'id's uncles and cousins began to abandon their support for Qais. Sa'id also became suspicious of Badr and his Saudi allies. Then in March 1806 Sa'id moved to free himself of his cousin's domination.

ACCESSION OF SA'ID IBN SULTAN

Sa'id loved to tell the story of how he took power in 1806. He told it to his Italian doctor and adviser, Vincenzo Maurizi, who then published it in a biography of the Sayyid. He told it to the Omani historian Humaid ibn Ruzaiq, who published it in his chronicle of Omani history. He even told it to an American ship captain who visited him in Zanzibar,

Muscat, c. 1890

Under Sa'id ibn Sultan (reigned 1806-56), Oman established friendship treaties with the United States (1833), France (1844), and strengthened its ties with Great Britain. In 1842 the Sayyid sent his ship, *The Sultana,* on a state visit to the United States. The ship's commander, Ahmad bin Na'aman Ka'abi, became the first envoy of any Arab country to reach the United States. He brought gifts of Omani stallions, a gold-handled sword, and a jar of rose water from the Jebel Akhdar. President John Tyler, in return, presented to Oman a collection of fine guns and a 24-pound cannon mounted as a field piece, each inscribed Saeed bin Sultan, 1258 A.H. in Arabic and then the English date: [A.D. 1842].

Muscat town, capital of Oman, long gave its name to the country, which was called Muscat and Oman until 1970. Fort Jalali is to the right and the sultan's palace is to the left.

and that ship captain wrote it in the log of his ship. He did love the story.

Sa'id did not always tell the same story. The historian ibn Ruzaiq claimed that Sa'id and Badr had gathered an army in Birka for an attack on their enemies. As they waited to meet their ally Muhammad ibn Nasir al-Jabri, the talk turned to daggers and swords. Sa'id drew his sword and pretended to attack Badr. The pretending then stopped, and Sa'id struck his uncle with his sword, and the

Sa'id next turned his attention to East Africa. Omani contact and interest in the Swahili Coast (modern Somalia to Mozambique) can be traced to ancient times when sailors from Arabia utilized the regular winds of the monsoon to sale back and forth across the Indian Ocean. While in Africa many Omanis married local women and established homes in coastal towns and islands. These "Swahili" (coastal) settlements developed a distinctive language and Muslim civilization with ties to both Africa and Arabia. The Ya'aribah imams assisted the Swahili settlements in expelling the Portuguese, and asserted political control for a time. During the political instability of the fall of the Ya'aribah and the early Al Bu Sa'id dynasties, Omani political control disappeared. Many Omanis emigrated to East Africa and established their own regimes in several of the ports. For example, the port of Mombasa was ruled by the Mazru'i family of Oman, while the island of Zanzibar, usually under governors from the Hinawi Bani Hirth tribe of the Sharqiyah, remained loyal to the Al Bu Sa'id.

However, before Sayyid Sa'id could turn his attention to East Africa, events in Oman required his attention. The Bani Bu Ali tribe of the Ja'alan region threatened Sayyid Sa'id transportation routes to the Swahili Coast. Therefore, in 1820 Sayyid invited the British to assist him in punishing the tribe. He used the pretext of piracy to persuade his European allies—despite the fact that the Bani Bu Ali had not been pirates. A first attack on the Bani Bu Ali failed, but the second succeeded in subduing the tribe. Sa'id appalled his allies by cutting down Bani Bu Ali palm trees and destroying their irrigation channels.

During 1821-1822, Sayyid Sa'id devoted nearly all of his attention to carving out an East African empire. Several Swahili ports fell to the Sayyid's forces. The inability to conquer Mombasa, the result of British interference, was the only failure of the campaign. After the British withdrew

Muscat Homes Facing Fort Jalali, 1905

These homes of the wealthy were located within the city wall. They were two and three storied surrounded by a courtyard. Inside walls were usually of plaster with ornately decorated white-plaster ceilings. The floors were covered with carpets and mats.

For centuries, Muscat was known for its maritime trade. Most of the wealthy were involved in some form of commerce. The population of Muscat in 1900 was about 25,000.

Today, Old Muscat is home to some fabulous old mosques and houses. Although they were at one time embassies and consulates, they are now museums.

from Mombasa, Sa'id's navy again attacked the port and defeated the Mazru'i. Unfortunately, once Sa'id's ships sailed over the horizon, the Mazru'i regained control of their town. In 1828 Sa'id made his first personal visit to East Africa and decided to make it his home. The next year he returned to Zanzibar to take up residence in his newly constructed palace and devote his full attention to an East African empire.

Sa'id's foreign adventures served to contribute to Muscat's increased importance as a commercial center. Sa'id himself was the principal merchant, and his navy transported goods as well as soldiers. Sa'id also actively recruited foreign merchants to settle in Muscat. During this period a number of Indian Hindu merchants, known as Banians, began to open businesses in the port. These Banians had important ties to both India and East Africa. Sa'id also utilized their accounting skills to manage his customs house, contracting with one or another of the Banian merchants to collect import duties. In addition to the Banians, merchants from Persia also settled in Muscat. The port prospered.

DIVISION IN OMAN

The period between 1814 and 1829 was a time of relative peace in Oman. The imam Sa'id resided peacefully in Rustaq until his death, possibly as late as 1821, when control of that town passed to Sayyid Sa'id. No election to replace the imam occurred. The fortunes of the Qais branch of the Al Bu Sa'id diminished greatly as the deaths of first Qais in 1808 and then his son in 1814 gave Sa'id control of Sohar. Sa'id also reconciled his differences with Muhammad ibn Nasir al-Jabri. Conditions in Oman were so secure that Sa'id performed the Muslim pilgrimage to Mecca in 1824.

Conditions changed after 1829. Sa'id departed Muscat for Zanzibar in December of that year, to return in June 1830. He remained in Muscat for 18 months but set sail for Zanzibar again in December 1831 and remained there for nearly a year. His next two visits lasted for nearly two years each, and then in December 1840 he began an 11-year absence in East Africa. He resided in Muscat for only 18 months in 1851-1852 before returning to Zanzibar. His final trip to Muscat came in the spring of 1854. Sa'id died while returning to Zanzibar in September 1856. During Sa'id's absences, control of Muscat passed to a regent, usually one of his sons or another close relative.

The Sayyid's long absences and the ineffective rule of his deputies provided opportunities for other family members to challenge the authority of Muscat in the rest of Oman. Once again opposition centered on the Qais branch of the Al Bu Sa'id. Sayyid Hamud ibn 'Azzan, grandson of Sayyid Qais ibn Ahmad, took immediate advantage of Sa'id's first trip to Zanzibar in 1830 to retake the town of Sohar and capture a number of other ports along the coast. Sa'id rushed back to Oman, reluctantly recognized Hamud's authority over Sohar, and left. Hamud's reputation and authority continued to grow at the expense of Sa'id, who only returned to Oman to quell major uprisings. Sa'id's position suffered even more with the death of powerful allies Muhammad ibn Nasir al-Jabri and his aunt Bibi Mawza. By the 1840s several of the Oman's religious leaders began promoting the election of Hamud as imam. Then in 1849 Sayyid Thuwaini ibn Sa'id, Sa'id's son and regent, imprisoned Hamud, who died soon after in a Muscat jail. Sa'id again returned from Zanzibar and completed the conquest of Sohar.

Hamud's death reduced the threat from the Qais branch of the Al Bu Sa'id, although the family remained in control of Rustaq. Sa'id returned to Zanzibar, making his final visit to Oman in 1854 when a Saudis invasion again threatened the country. Once that threat subsided, the Sayyid boarded a ship for East Africa. It was his last voyage, for he died near the Seychelles Islands.

Omani Sheikhs, 1930

"Sheikh" is an Arabic title of respect dating from pre-Islamic antiquity. It usually refers to a venerable man of more than 50 years of age. The title sheikh is also used by tribal chiefs as well as by any man who has memorized the entire Koran, however young he might be.

3

The Al Bu Sa'id Struggle for Power

Sayyid Sa'id ibn Sultan's death in 1856 resulted in a power struggle that continued until the mid-1950s, for the loss of this strong, dynamic individual reopened the whole question of the nature of rule in Oman. Most importantly, the desire for a reestablishment of imamate government re-emerged. For most of the 19th century that struggle occurred principally within the confines of the Al Bu Sa'id royal family.

POLITICAL FRAGMENTATION

Sayyid Thuwaini ibn Sa'id peacefully succeeded his father in 1856, but he exercised very minimal control over Oman. His principal opposition came from within the Al Bu Sa'id royal family. Thuwaini's brother Sayyid Turki ibn Sa'id ruled Sohar, while his distant cousins Sayyid Qais ibn 'Azzan (d.1861) and then Qais' son Sayyid 'Azzan ibn Qais resided in Rustaq. Other Al Bu Sa'id held strategic forts throughout the country. Newly emerging tribal tamimahs and religious leaders also required Thuwaini's attention. Salih ibn Ali al-Harithi ruled much of the Sharqiyah region as well as claiming the allegiance of the Hinawi tribes. The Ibadi scholar Sa'id ibn Khalfan al-Khalili, an ally of Qais ibn 'Azzan, actively supported the election of an imam. Additionally, the Saudis continued to pressure Oman from their base in the Buraimi oasis. Finally, Sayyid Thuwaini also sought to maintain Omani control over Zanzibar where his brother Sayyid Majid ibn Sa'id served as governor.

The new ruler of Muscat met with limited success. Thuwaini submitted the matter of Zanzibar to British mediation. The resulting Canning Award (1861) declared Muscat and Zanzibar to be separate sultanates but required that Sultan Majid of Zanzibar yearly pay 40,000 Maria Theresa dollars—a large Austrian silver coin used widely in the Indian Ocean region during this period—to Thuwaini in compensation. In Oman Thuwaini seized Sohar from his brother in 1861. Qais ibn 'Azzan then launched a revolt against Sultan Thuwaini. Qais died in the conflict, but his son 'Azzan succeeded in maintaining control of the towns captured by his father. In 1864 Thuwaini attempted to recover that territory and take Rustaq from 'Azzan ibn Qais. Saudi intervention preserved 'Azzan's position but rallied Omani tribal support behind Sultan Thuwaini. Great Britain also became a strong supporter of Thuwaini, providing naval assistance against the sultan's enemies. In January 1866 Sultan

Fortress at Rustaq, 1885

This fortress was built around an ancient 7th-century stronghold in the early 17th century.

Rustaq is an oaisis in northern Oman about 96 miles southwest of Muscat and some 40 miles from the coast. En route to India, the Portuguese had gained control over most of Oman by 1508. They were driven from the area in 1650.

In 1885 the Rustaq oasis had a population of about 14,000 people. It owed much of its reputation to its thermal springs, known for centuries. The fortress is the oldest inhabited building in this part of the Arabian peninsula. In recent years the Omani government has restored the fort and its towers.

Wherever one goes in Oman, there is a constant reminder of the country's past—from massive forts to small watchtowers that cluster atop most mountains. Generally, forts protected towns and populated areas, while watchtowers guarded inland trade routes.

Thuwaini, with the assistance of Salih ibn Ali al-Harithi and Sayyid Turki, gathered his forces in Sohar to attack the Saudi stronghold at Buraimi. Before the invasion could be launched, however, Thuwaini died, shot in the head by his son Sayyid Salim in February 1866.

Despite the patricide, the British extended immediate recognition to Salim ibn Thuwaini as sultan of Muscat. Other Omanis did not agree. Sayyid Turki quickly raised an army to overthrow Salim. Only British intervention prevented him from capturing Muscat and expelling Salim. Salim then sought to imprison Salih ibn Ali al-Harithi, but Salih escaped and fled to Rustaq to encourage Sayyid 'Azzan to yet another revolt against Muscat. 'Azzan, with the support of Sa'id ibn Khalfan al-Khalili, seized the opportunity. Salih ibn Ali returned to the Sharqiyah to raise the Hirth and other Hinawi tribes against the sultan. Rebel forces marched on Muscat in September 1868 and invited Salim to accept the guidance of the ulema in administering his state. Salim refused. On October 1 Muscat fell, although Salim held out in one of Muscat's forts, hoping for the arrival of British gunboats. Those gunboats arrived—but to carry Sultan Salim ibn Thuwaini off into exile rather than preserve his throne.

THE IMAMATE OF 'AZZAN IBN QAIS

'Azzan's capture of Muscat marked a victory for the Qais branch in the conflict within the Al Bu Sa'id that dated back to the death of Imam Ahmad ibn Sa'id in 1783. With the overthrow of the sultanate, the new regime sought to implement the Ibadi ideal. Sa'id ibn Khalfan al-Khalili convened a committee of religious and tribal leaders, the latter dominated by Salih ibn Ali al-Harithi, and duly elected Sayyid 'Azzan ibn Qais Al

Bu Sa'id as imam. For the religious leaders such as Sa'id ibn Khalfan al-Khalili, 'Azzan's election represented an Ibadi *nahda* (renaissance) in which political authority once again resided in a righteous imam who would "decree what is lawful and prohibit what is unlawful."

The unification of Oman followed very rapidly thereafter. Although the Hinawi tribes actively supported the new imamate, the Ghafiri tribes, and in particular the Bani Riyam under their powerful tamimah (tribal leader) Saif ibn Sulaiman al-Nabhani, had remained neutral in the conflict. 'Azzan first turned his attention to the defeat of the tribes of the Ja'alan, who were mostly Sunni, and the final expulsion of the Saudi forces from Buraimi. Those two campaigns concluded by the end of the summer of 1869. During the fall of that year 'Azzan next directed his military and diplomatic efforts to the Omani heartland around Nizwa. Final victory came when Saif ibn Sulaiman al-Nabhani proclaimed his submission to the imam—his statement coming during the duress of imprisonment while visiting 'Azzan ibn Qais under the protection of a safe-conduct pass.

However, Omanis, unified for the first time in almost a century, were not content with the imamate. Ghafiri tribes resented the imposition of a Hinawi imam, and the Bani Riyam chafed at the treachery demonstrated toward their tamimah. There was also economic fallout when customs revenues in Muscat fell dramatically because the imam's supporters persecuted the port's Hindu merchant community. Much in need of resources, 'Azzan ibn Qais began confiscating the property of supporters of the sultanate. When those sources dried up, the imam stopped paying soldiers recruited from loyal tribes and made increased demands for money from his own supporters. Now even the Hinawi tribes became dissatisfied.

Indigo Vat Dyeing, Nizwa, 1901

Indigo was known to the ancients. The blue dye was made by boiling indigo plants outdoors in large vats. Unlike other natural dyes, indigo is not water-soluble and it was difficult to get the color to adhere to the cotton cloth that was added to the vats—hence, the term "vat dyeing."

In 1880 Adolf von Baeyer, a German chemist, synthesized indigo and formulated its structure. This made possible the manufacturing of a commercial substance that eventually replaced the procedure in this photograph. For his work, Baeyer was awarded the 1905 Nobel Prize for Chemistry.

Sayyid Turki began organizing opposition to the imamate. With financial support from family members in Zanzibar, Turki gathered forces in the Dhahirah region in September 1870. Saif ibn Sulaiman al-Nabhani joined with Turki and in the winter of 1870-1871 and led the Bani Riyam and other Ghafiri tribes in revolt. In January 1871 Turki divided his forces in half, sending Saif ibn Sulaiman and his followers to attack Muscat while his army marched to the Sharqiyah to attack the Hirth of Salih ibn Ali. By the end of the month, Muscat fell; both 'Azzan ibn Qais and Saif ibn Sulaiman al-Nabhani died during the battle. Sa'id ibn Khalfan al-Khalili died in prison three months later, buried alive on the orders of Sultan Turki.

THE SULTANATES OF TURKI IBN SA'ID AND FAISAL IBN TURKI

Although Turki quickly obtained British recognition as sultan of Muscat, he ruled only over the port. Salih ibn Ali al-Harithi remained firmly in control of the Sharqiyah and the Hinawi confederation. Sayyid Ibrahim ibn Qais, the dead imam's brother, captured Rustaq and Sohar in the chaos of the civil war. The ulema' resented the treachery against their leader Sa'id ibn Khalfan al-Khalili. The Saudis had also taken advantage of Oman's instability to reoccupy Buraimi. Finally, other family members, such as former sultan Salim ibn Thuwaini and Turki's brother 'Abd al-'Aziz ibn Sa'id, aspired to be sultan. Only the new tamimah of the Bani Riyam, Sulaiman ibn Saif al-Nabhani, supported the sultan, but his support depended entirely on the money that Sultan Turki could pay him.

Turki's reign (1871-1888) was, therefore, a constant struggle to maintain control of at least his capital. Salih ibn 'Ali and Ibrahim ibn Qais cooperated repeatedly in efforts to overthrow the sultanate and reestablish an Al Bu Sa'id imamate under Ibrahim. Only British intervention prevented this from happening. Fortunately for Turki, by the early 1880s both Salih ibn Ali and Ibrahim ibn Qais had become weary of the struggle and unhappy with each other.

The one notable success of Sultan Turki's reign was the establishment of Muscati control over Dhofar. Sayyid Sa'id had occupied the town of Salalah in 1829. Despite claims of sovereignty, he and his successors had not ruled the region. During the 1870s one Fadhl ibn Alawi, an Indian Muslim immigrant, claimed to be the ruler of Dhofar on behalf of the Ottoman Empire. Sultan Turki encouraged the Bait Kathir tribe of Dhofar to revolt against Fadhl ibn Alawi, an idea that they supported because of the ruler's diligent collection of taxes. In 1879 the Bait Kathir succeeded in expelling Fadhl ibn Alawi, and Sultan Turki immediately sent his own governor. A Bait Kathir revolt against the sultan expelled his governor in 1885, but Sayyid Turki reasserted control just before his death in June 1888.

Sultan Turki's death brought to the throne in Muscat his son Faisal ibn Turki, the first ruler of the 19th century to succeed peacefully. Sultan Faisal sought actively to assert his control over all of Oman. The policy began with an unsuccessful attack on Sayyid Ibrahim ibn Qais in Rustaq, and Faisal's failure served only to diminish what little reputation the sultan had. Next he interfered in tribal politics by trying to have Salih ibn Ali replaced as tamimah of the Hirth. When Salih ibn Ali learned of the plot, he gathered his forces and very easily occupied Muscat in 1895. Ghafiri support and British intervention once again saved the sultan of Muscat. With his delusions of grandeur dimmed, Sultan Faisal turned his attentions away from interior Oman

Sultan Faysal Ibn Turki, c. 1908

Sultan Faysal ibn Turki (reigned 1888-1913) was the great-grandfather of the present sultan of Oman.

During Faysal ibn Turki's rule, the authority of the sultan declined in the Oman interior, requiring periodic British assistance to supress revolts.

to concentrate on strengthening the defenses of Muscat against tribal attack and consolidating his position in Dhofar.

MUSCAT: THE GLOBAL CITY

While the politics of Oman were marked with continued instability and violence, the city of Muscat continued to develop as an important trade center for both Oman and the western Indian Ocean region. During the second half of the 19th century it could well claim to be a global city, with an international population trading with the rest of the world and taking advantage of technological innovations such as the telegraph and steamship transportation.

An important change that occurred in Muscat during the time after Sayyid Sa'id was the growing role of foreigners in the port's trade. Sa'id had always utilized the services of Hindu merchants, the Banians, most of who came from the Kutch area of western India. In the late 19th century, Banians such as Ratansi Purshottam came to dominate this trade—however, the Banians dominated but did not monopolize Muscat's trade. During these years Muscat became home to an international population. Shi'ite Muslims from India, known as the Luwatiyah, rose to prominence in the city of Matrah. Arab traders such as Yusuf al-Zawawi opened businesses in Muscat. Various other nationalities including Baluchi, French, English, and even a few Americans became active in the market.

These merchants were not mere transient residents. Most of the larger Banian merchants owned homes and settled their families in Muscat. The community also operated two temples in the port and had their own graveyard. W. J. Towell Company, owned by the Luwatiyah Al-Sultan family, eventually became one of the largest commercial houses in the Persian Gulf. The Luwatiyah also had their own mosques and other institutions. American missionaries of the Dutch Reformed Church of America also took up residence in Muscat in 1890, founding their own church, opening a school and a clinic, and operating—for a very short time—the first printing press in Oman. Their missionaries often ventured out to spread the word of Jesus in interior Oman, although with no success.

Muscat served as an entrepôt, a distribution center. Slaves from East Africa had been a major commodity during the early years under discussion, but the British suppressed this trade by the 1860s. Omani dates became an important export item. American merchants bought tons of this product for sale during the Thanksgiving and Christmas holidays in the United States. Muscat also served as the major distribution center for arms in the western Indian Ocean and South Asian region. European merchants, representing the main firearms manufacturers in England, Germany, Belgium, and France, supplied trading houses in Muscat with the latest weapons and ammunition for sale in Oman, neighboring Arab states, Iran, Afghanistan, and India.

Muscat benefited greatly from technological innovations of the late 19th century. During the 1860s regular steamship service linked Europe and India, and these ships began to include Muscat in their routes. While the bigger, faster steamships harmed the traditional trade carried by Omani sailing craft, they did serve to increase Muscat's contacts with the wider world. Then in 1901 Muscat became linked to the global telegraph system, and the city's merchants began to utilize this rapid form of communication to conduct business all around the world.

END OF AN ERA

During the early years of the 20th century, Oman began to undergo major changes. Sultan Faisal suffered through serious illnesses throughout most of this time and was unable to devote his full attentions to governing his state. In addition, Britain came to exercise considerable influence on Muscati affairs. Finally, a new generation of tribal and religious leaders emerged in interior Oman to challenge the existing political situation.

Since 1856 the British had become the guarantors of the independence of the sultans of Muscat. Only direct intervention on various occasions had prevented the Omanis from reestablishing an imamate under one of the relatives of 'Azzan ibn Qais. Furthermore, British intercession to end the slave and arms trade from Muscat served only to alienate important tribal leaders such as Sulaiman ibn Saif al-Nabhani and the Ghafiri tribes that had usually supported the sultans. Then in 1891 the British strengthened their influence in Muscat. Formal relations between Muscat and England were based on an 1839 commercial treaty. In renegotiating that treaty in 1891 Britain included a secret provision in which Sultan Faisal promised ". . . never to cede, to sell, to mortgage or otherwise give for occupation save to the British government, the dominions of Muscat and Oman . . ." Muscat became a virtual British protectorate.

Meanwhile, major leadership changes occurred in interior Oman. As already mentioned, Himyar ibn Sulaiman al-Nabhani, traditionally a supporter of the sultanate, had become increasingly alienated by British trade policies. Other changes included the emergence of a new generation of tribal and religious leaders. Salih ibn Ali al-Harithi died in 1896, to be replaced by his son 'Isa ibn Salih al-Harithi as tamimah of the Hirth and leader of the

Hinawis. Himyar ibn Sulaiman al-Nabhani was murdered in 1889 and was succeeded by his nephew Himyar ibn Nasir al-Nabhani. A year before, in 1898, Ibrahim ibn Qais Al Bu Sa'id died. Sa'ud ibn 'Azzan ibn Qais, son of the last imam, sought to secure his own election as imam. His murder in 1899 ended not only his effort but also left the Al Bu Sa'id without a candidate for the office. Finally, a new generation of religious leaders—most notably the blind legal scholar Abdullah ibn Humaid al-Salimi, a student of Salih ibn Ali al-Harithi—began actively working toward a restoration of the imamate ideal.

Sultan Sa'id Ibn Taimur, 1905

Sultan Sa'id ibn Taimur (reigned 1932-70) was the father of the present sultan of Oman.

Sa'id ibn Taimur's father, Sultan Taimur ibn Faisal (reigned 1913-31), was allowed to abdicate by complicated Anglo-Omani manuvering to end his rule.

Sultan Sa'id ibn Taimur, according to a British adviser was "an arch-reactionary of great personal charm." He wanted no change of any sort in Oman and he did all the he could to isolate his country from the world. All visas were personally issued by him. He forbade travel to the interior by coastal residents and vice versa. He opposed education for his subjects, believing it a threat to his power.

The sultan's only contact with the outside world was through his British advisors and Muscat's merchant families. In exchange for their lucrative monopolies,

the merchant families stayed out of politics. They imported nothing that Sultan Sa'id felt reeked of the West, such as radios and books. However, most of the population relied upon agriculture and fishing for subsistence.

4

Sultanate
and Imamate

n 1913 the Omanis selected a new imam, and a new era began in the history of the country as Muscat and Oman came to be ruled by separate governments, a circumstance formalized by the Treaty of Sib in 1920. Two imams, Salim ibn Rashid al-Kharusi (1913-1920) and Muhammad b. Abdullah al-Khalili (1920-1954), and two sultans, Taimur ibn Faisal Al-Sa'id (1913-1931) and Said ibn Taimur Al-Sa'id (1931-1970), reigned until the 1950s. Muscat and Oman also experienced a serious economic decline brought about by the disruptions of World War I, the global depression of the 1930s, and then World War II.

IMAMATE RESTORED AND THE "TREATY OF SIB"

The year 1913 represents a turning point in Omani history. By that year the principal tribal confederations of the interior, the Ghafiri under Himyar b. Nasir al-Nabhani, tamimah of the Bani Riyam, the Hinawi under Isa ibn Salih al-Harithi, tamimah of the Bani Hirth, and the Ibadi religious establishment, under the great blind theologian and historian Abdullah ibn Humaid al-Salimi, had united in opposition to Al Bu Sa'id political dominance in Oman. In May Himyar ibn Nasir and Abdullah ibn Humaid al-Salimi convened a meeting in Himyar's hometown of Tanuf to elect Salim ibn Rashid al-Kharusi imam and to declare that Sultan Faisal ibn Turki was deposed. Isa ibn Salih al-Harithi ignored the invitation to what he considered to be a Ghafiri conclave.

Imamate forces quickly captured the major towns of the interior and prepared to advance on the coast. Isa ibn Salih al-Harithi now joined with the imamate. Tragically, Sultan Faisal became ill and died in October, to be succeeded by his son Sayyid Taimur b. Faisal. The British notified the imam that they would not permit the fall of Muscat and sent Indian troops to defend the port. During 1914, imamate forces continued to advance along the Batinah coast, and only British naval bombardment permitted Sultan Taimur to retain control over coastal towns close to his capital. Then in January 1915 the long-anticipated attack on Muscat came. The Indian troops supplied by Taimur's British protectors easily repulsed the attack before it posed a serious threat to the city.

The next several years witnessed intermittent fighting and negotiations between the two sides. Sultan Taimur's army managed to re-conquer the Batinah coast, but the imamate held the interior. The sultan also imposed punitive taxes of 25 percent on all dates brought from interior Oman to the coast, greatly hurting farmers under the imam's authority. Discussions to resolve the conflict failed.

Circumstances changed dramatically in 1920 when in February, Himyar b. Nasir al-Nabhani died, to be succeeded by his 13-year-old son, Sulaiman b. Himyar, as tamimah of the Bani Riyam. Imam Salim ibn Rashid died at the hand of an assassin in July. Abdullah ibn Humaid al-Salimi had already died in 1914. Muhammad ibn Abdullah al-Khalili, tamimah of the Hinawi Bani Ruwahah, the grandson of the great 19th century supporter of the imamate Sa'id ibn Khalfan al-Khalili and a close ally of 'Isa ibn Salih al-Harithi, secured election as the new imam.

The new leadership in interior Oman proved to be more accepting of an agreement. In September, Isa ibn Salih al-Harithi, representing the imam, and the British Political Agent in Muscat, Ronald Wingate, representing the sultan, negotiated a settlement. The so-called Treaty of Sib set the basis for relations between Muscat and Oman until the early 1950s. According to the exchange of letters, each side promised not to interfere in the affairs of the other and to allow free trade and travel between each other's territories. Sultan Taimur ibn Faisal did not renounce his claim to be the ruler of all of Oman; Imam Muhammad ibn Abdullah al-Khalili did not recognize the sovereignty of the sultanate.

MUSCAT AND OMAN

For the next decade, interior Oman grew increasingly isolated under Imam Muhammad ibn Abdullah. Isa ibn Salih al-Harithi and Sulaiman ibn Himyar al-Nabhani remained the dominant political figures. The two often competed for influence, as in 1925 when Isa ibn Salih raised a force to counter a Saudi threat in Buraimi and Sulaiman ibn Himyar threatened to attack Nizwa if the Hinawi force proceeded.

Under British pressure, Sultan Taimur ibn Faisal

Omani from the "Interior," c. 1930

The section of Oman historically known as the "Interior" refers to
the region lying beyond the al-Hajar Mountains where, from fortified
strongholds, the local imams contested the authority of the sultan in
Muscat. Hence, the name "Muscat and Oman" to describe the country
prior to 1970.

In this area dwelled several nomadic tribes whose lives and
customs remained untouched until the advent of the oil economy
in the 1960's.

Al-Sa'id began to modernize the Muscati state. Finances were the primary concern as the Sultan was indebted to nearly every merchant in Muscat. In exchange for British control of finances, Sultan Taimur received a loan from the British government and paid off those debts. Bertram Thomas—later to become famous as an Arabian traveler—became the finance minister. Other affairs were handled by a four-member Council of Ministers, headed by Sayyid Nadir ibn Faisal Al-Said, the sultan's brother. The other major reform was the creation of the Muscat Levy Corps, a full-time army with Baluchi soldiers and British officers.

Sultan Taimur proved to be a reluctant monarch, spending most of his days in Salalah in Dhofar or India or traveling, all the time expressing his desire to resign as sultan. The British had almost to force him to periodically visit Muscat. In his absence, the Council of Ministers ruled the state. Beginning in 1929, when he returned from school in India and Iraq, Crown Prince Sayyid Sa'id ibn Taimur began to play a central role in the governing of Muscat.

Few major problems faced the government. A major threat did arise in 1923 when Muhammad ibn Nasir, the tamimah of the Bani Bu Ali of the Ja'alan region, proclaimed his independence, going so far as to raise a flag and issuing travel documents. The death of Muhammad in 1929 did not fully resolve the matter, and it took the threat of British aerial bombardment to force his son to formally recognize sultanate authority. Other tribal uprisings in the Batinah and Masandam—again met with British gunboats—proved less threatening.

SA'ID IBN TAIMUR

Sultan Taimur finally received his wish in November 1931 when he was allowed to resign. Sa'id ibn Taimur immediately succeeded him, although the British refused to recognize his position until February 1932. The new sultan then set out to free himself of British control. His first act was to end the service of Bertram Thomas. (Thomas proved to be much more interested in establishing a reputation as an Arabian explorer in the Masandam Peninsula and the Rub al-Khali Desert than in managing Muscat's meager finances, anyway.) British officials in India and London sought to impose a new British financial adviser on Sultan Sa'id, but he refused and took direct control of state accounts.

The meagerness of those accounts posed the greatest challenge for the sultan. The first blow to Muscat's economy came with the outbreak of World War I. Although Oman did not participate directly in the conflict, ships stopped calling at the port, thus ending vital imports and exports. Oman's revenues, based on tariffs on imports and tax on agricultural production, plummeted. Trade recovered slightly after the war but virtually ended during the world-wide depression of the 1930s. Despite these difficulties, Sa'id managed to maintain a balanced budget and keep his state out of debt.

Administration remained limited. Sa'id replaced his father's Council of Ministers with a group of three close advisers. Sayyid Ahmad ibn Ibrahim Al Bu Sa'id, a member of the Qais branch of the royal family, served as minister of the Interior. His duties included administering the court system, which included religious judges overseeing applica-tion of the Shari'a, and the provincial administration of the sultanate's governors in the principal towns. Ahmad ibn Ibrahim also played an important role in maintaining close relations between Sultan Sa'id and the tribal leaders, especially the tamimahs of the major tribes such as the Hirth and the Bani Riyam.

Sa'id's uncle, Sayyid Shihab ibn Faisal Al-Sa'id, served as "Ceremonial Representative of the Sultan," a kind of deputy sultan. His various duties included administering the

Muscat/Matrah municipality, supervision of the police and jails, command of the sultanate's army, the Muscat Infantry, and directing the one government-operated school.

The third minister was Hamud ibn Hamad al-Ghafiri, the governor of Dhofar. Although Sultan Sa'id ruled the southern province as a personal fiefdom, Hamud ibn Hamad's duties in Dhofar generally coincided with those of both Sayyids Ahmad and Shihab in northern Oman.

Other family members played important roles in the administration. Sultan Sa'id's two younger brothers, Sayyids Tariq ibn Taimur and Fahr ibn Taimur served in the Muscat Infantry, and Sayyid Tariq also administered the municipality for a time. Sayyid Shihab's son Sayyid Thuwaini ibn Shihab was his father's deputy, and a nephew, Sayyid Faisal ibn Ali Al-Sa'id, was a translator and Arabic teacher in the school. Two prominent personal advisers to the Sultan were Zubair ibn Ali al-Hutti, the former justice minister, and Abd al-Munim ibn Yusuf al-Zawawi, an important merchant who served as a foreign representative in India and Pakistan.

With limited financial means, there was little for the government to administer. Most development focused on the "capital area" around Muscat and Matrah, where automobiles were introduced and paved roads constructed. Graded roads linked Muscat with important coastal villages and towns. The Muscat and Matrah municipality also developed telephone, electrical, sanitation and water systems for the capital area. Education remained a community affair, with traditional Koran schools providing most instruction. American Christian missionaries and the local Indian communities also operated elementary schools. The government, on the other hand, administered one elementary school for boys in Muscat. Health care was almost nonexistent outside the American mission hospital in Matrah and the government hospital in Muscat.

Sultan Sa'id sought to broaden his state's financial resources. Fisheries and agricultural surveys in both Dhofar and along the Batinah coast occurred following World War II, but the greatest promise was oil. Sa'id contacted the Arabian American Oil Company, but the British informed the sultan that any agreement required their approval. Sultan Sa'id then concluded an agreement with the Iraq Petroleum Company, which created a subsidiary that came to be called Petroleum Development Oman (PDO) Ltd. for exploration in Oman and Dhofar. The imamate denied access to the territories in interior Oman, and World War II ended oil exploration activities and delayed the promise of oil wealth.

Meanwhile, conditions in the imamate were equally difficult. Imam Muhammad ibn Abdullah al-Khalili was ill during much of the 1940s, a condition that only contributed to his isolation from affairs in Oman and the wider world. 'Isa ibn Salih al-Harithi, loyal to the imam but following an independent policy, maintained friendly relations with Sultan Sa'id, often visiting him in Muscat. Furthermore, most of Oman was ravaged by a severe drought that devastated agriculture, the main source of state revenues. World War II only served to aggravate the situation, as Oman's exports found no markets and rice imports became very dear due to wartime shortages and rationing. Many Omanis, especially from the Sharqiyah region, began to emigrate to Zanzibar or, in the immediate postwar era, to the northern sheikhdoms in Kuwait, Bahrain, and the Trucial Coast.

The political balance in the interior was also disrupted when 'Isa ibn Salih al-Harithi died in 1946. 'Isa's son and successor died within a year, resulting in a power struggle between another of Isa's sons Salih ibn 'Isa al-Harithi and a grandson, Ahmad ibn Muhammad al-Harithi. Salih emerged victorious—but at the expense of tribal unity. Ahmad ibn Muhammad began seeking the favor of Sultan

Muscat Street Scene, 1940
The city wall can be seen in the upper left of this photograph.

Sa'id. With Harithi influence weakened, Sulaiman ibn Himyar al-Nabhani emerged as the dominant secular power in the imamate.

The interwar period was a time of hardship for most Omanis. The shared administrations of sultan and imam provided general security for their populations, but meager financial resources permitted little else. Relations between the two administrations were also generally cordial, each respecting the role of the other. Early in the 1950s, all of these conditions began to change.

Sa'id ibn Taimur, c. 1940

Photograph of Sa'id ibn Taimur, the sultan of Muscat and Oman, taken in 1940.

5

Unification and Opposition

By 1952 a series of challenges began to emerge that threatened the long-term stability of Oman. Much of what happened focused on oil, but the political instability of interior Oman and the imamate and the increasingly repressive nature of the rule of Sa'id ibn Taimur also contributed to the instability. This series of events began with the Saudi Arabian occupation of Buraimi in 1952 and included Sa'id ibn Taimur's efforts to eliminate the imamate and the subsequent civil war, the exploration, discovery, and production of oil, and the Dhofar war.

Diplomatic maneuvering dominated much of the next year. The imamate sought more formal legal existence by applying for admission to the Arab League and issuing of its own passports. Sultan Sa'id also became more active, ending his two-year isolation in Salalah to return to Muscat and begin discussions with major tribal leaders, most notably Ahmad ibn Muhammad al-Harithi. Even Sulaiman ibn Himyar traveled to Muscat to meet with the sultan.

Then in the spring of 1955 sultanate military forces discovered secret Saudi arms shipments to the imam. Finally in October the British agreed to military action against the Saudis in Buraimi. The Muscat and Oman Field Force marched from 'Ibri to Buraimi, taking control of a number of interior towns in the process. The Muscati army and Trucial Oman Scouts from Dubai expelled Saudi forces with little difficulty. In December the sultan's forces turned to the south, easily occupying Nizwa after imam Ghalib fled to the protection of a powerful relative and announced his retirement. Salih ibn 'Isa al-Harithi and other leaders of the imamate fled to Saudi Arabia. Sa'id, having recently returned to Salalah, quickly traveled to Nizwa to accept the allegiance of the tribal leaders, most notably Ahmad ibn Muhammad al-Harithi, the new tamimah of the Bani Hirth, and Sulaiman ibn Himyar al-Nabhani. Oman was united in a single government.

THE RESTORATION MOVEMENT AND CIVIL WAR

Sultan Sa'id did little to consolidate his control over Oman. After a brief visit to Muscat, he returned to Salalah. Ahmad ibn Muhammad al-Harithi became the virtual ruler of Sharqiyah while Sulaiman ibn Himyar al-Nabhani remained under surveillance in Muscat. Then in May 1957, just a year and a half after unification, the sultan did little to suppress an uprising by the Harithi supporters of the imamate. Many of those who had fled to Saudi Arabia in 1955 filtered back into Oman. Then in June Ghalib ibn Ali proclaimed the restoration of the imamate. The sultan ordered an attack on the imam's home, but it failed. Sulaiman ibn Himyar left Muscat to return to interior Oman and rally the Bani Riyam in support of Imam Ghalib.

Sultan Sa'id's control of Oman deteriorated rapidly. His army withdrew to the oil company base at Fahud. The imam's followers reoccupied Nizwa and most of the principal towns of the interior. Great Britain immediately sent Royal Air Force and British regular army units to reinforce Omani forces. During the month of August, most of the sultan's losses were recovered. Imam Ghalib and Sulaiman ibn Himyar withdrew to the mountainous plateau of al-Jabal al-Akhdar. The difficult approaches to the mountain made their position virtually impregnable, although they were still able to receive supplies from their Saudi allies. From this vantage point, supporters of the imam launched a guerrilla-warfare campaign by mining roads and attacking military convoys and oil company operations in the region below the mountain.

Sultan Sa'id's military forces lacked both the man-power and resources to dislodge the imam's forces, especially because his British allies withdrew after the initial victory in 1955. Accordingly, in January 1958, Sa'id again sought direct British assistance. A new agreement established British control over the sultan's armed forces and British guidance in an economic development program. Under the command of a British officer, the Sultan's Armed Forces (SAF) were reorganized, trained, and provided with modern equipment in preparation for the conquest of al-Jabal al-Akhdar.

Disputed Oman, 1957

In August of 1957 British and Muscat troops captured a fort in Nizwa
to reinforce Sultan Sa'id's control over Oman.

SAF also received assistance from the British Special Air Services (SAS), an elite special-operations unit.

The final assault began in December 1958. SAF proved unable to expel the enemy from the mountain, and another squadron of SAS troops came to their assistance. Finally in January 1959 resistance on the mountain ended as the imam's forces surrendered. Imam Ghalib ibn Ali and Sulaiman ibn Himyar both managed to escape to Saudi Arabia. Supporters of the imamate continued to plant a few mines through 1960, but the leaderless revolt soon ended. Oman was again unified under the rule of Sultan Sa'id.

SA'ID'S FINAL YEARS: PROMISE AND DESPAIR

Sultan Sa'id's next several years were devoted to consolidating control over Oman as he strengthened his alliances with major tribes such as the Bani Hirth and the Bani Hina'i. A new development office, under British control and with British financing, began expanding on initiatives, including medical dispensaries in Nizwa and Sur and a new school in Sur, already undertaken by the sultan. New roads linked Muscat with both the coastal city of Sohar and the Sharqiyah region, and 20 new health centers opened around the country. The development office also sought to improve agriculture in Oman with experimental farms in Sohar and Nizwa.

Greater development depended on oil revenues. Despite nearly seven years of frustration, PDO finally discovered oil in its fifth test well in September 1962 at Yibal. Further discoveries followed at Natih in 1963 and at Fahud in 1964. Production was delayed until the completion of a pipeline from Fahud to a new oil terminal at Mina al-Fahl. Exports finally began in August 1967. During the previous year, Sa'id contracted a consultant to prepare a development scheme, to include a girls' school, housing, government offices, a water system, and a new hospital for the capital area of Muscat. Then in January 1968 the sultan issued a proclamation on future development of a modern port, and airport, electrification, and improved water resources. Unfortunately, Sa'id had spent too many years without money, and although plans were made and contracts issued, he proved reluctant to actually spend his newfound wealth. The development schemes progressed very slowly.

In the meantime, new problems began to emerge for Sultan Sa'id. While Oman began to open up to the wider world, foreign affairs remained firmly under the control of the British. India opened a consulate in Muscat, and West Germany began the process of establishing diplomatic relations. However, Imam Ghalib, from his exile in Saudi Arabia and Iraq, had been very active in courting Arab support for his claims to control in Oman. "Progressive" Arab states such as Egypt and Iraq joined with conservative regimes in Saudi Arabia to bring the "Oman Question" first to the Arab League and then to the United Nations General Assembly. Sultan Sa'id found himself under the international spotlight in a most unfavorable glow. He refused to cooperate with the world body in what he considered to be a purely internal matter.

Sultan Sa'id became more and more isolated, and those around him—both British and Omani—became more and more frustrated. After a brief trip to Muscat in 1958, he returned to Salalah, never to visit his capital again. The sultan also attempted to prevent Omanis from leaving the country, no doubt fearing that they would join the opposition centering on Imam Ghalib and his Arab allies. But leave they did. Most Omani subjects left for simple economic reasons, seeking jobs in Saudi

Arabia, Kuwait, and the Trucial States of Abu Dhabi and Dubai. Others sought educational opportunities in Egypt, the United States, Western Europe, and countries of the former Soviet bloc.

The exiles also included a number of prominent family members. Sayyid Tariq ibn Taimur, the sultan's capable younger brother, left in frustration in 1960, eventually settling in Germany. Several cousins left Oman, including Sayyid Faisal ibn Ali (who went to Egypt) and Sayyid Fahd ibn Mahmud (who settled in France), thus denying Sa'id important personal resources and support.

While many Omanis left, others sought more direct opposition to Sa'id's repression. The greatest threat came from the Dhofar region of southern Oman. From his palace in Salalah, Sa'id ruled Dhofar as a personal fiefdom. The local population suffered from grinding poverty, eking out an existence on fishing, farming, and cattle raising. When they did not pay their taxes, Sa'id imposed economic restrictions that prohibited trade with Salalah and launched punitive raids with his army. Dissatisfaction turned to desperation and anger.

Armed opposition to Sa'id began in 1962 when a small group of Bait Kathir blew up an oil company exploration vehicle and began firing on SAF units operating in their territory. A government counterattack succeeded in capturing the leader of the uprising, Musallim ibn Nufl, but he escaped to Iraq. Also in 1962 a group of Dhofari nationalists formed the Dhofar Liberation Front (DLF). With assistance from both Egypt and Iraq, the DLF began a guerrilla war against Sultan Sa'id in 1964. In April 1966 a group of Sa'id's bodyguards loyal to the DLF almost succeeded in assassinating the sultan. Sa'id retaliated by ordering the construction of a barbed-wire fence around Salalah, thus completely closing off the city to the rest of Dhofar.

Conditions only deteriorated further. In 1967 the British colony of South Arabia (formerly Aden and the Eastern and Western Protectorates) became the independent People's Democratic Republic of Yemen (more commonly known as South Yemen) with the Middle East's only Marxist government. The DLF now had a much more secure source of both psychological and military support. The movement went on the offensive, occupying the towns of Madhub and Rakhyut, and by the summer of 1969 controlled most of western Dhofar.

By 1968, however, divisions had begun to occur within the DLF. The Dhofari nationalists, such as Musallim ibn Nufl and Yusuf ibn al-Alawi, found themselves outnumbered by Marxists with a more internationalist ideology. The Marxists, lead by Muhammad al-Ghassani, assumed control of the revolution under the new name Popular Front for the Liberation of the Arabian Gulf (PFLOAG). With a regular flow of supplies from its South Yemeni allies through the occupied port in Rakhyut and regular support from Iraq, the People's Republic of China, and the Soviet bloc, PFLOAG made rapid gains. By the spring of 1970 Sa'id controlled little beyond Salalah and the military base at Thumrait.

As Sa'id's British military advisers debated with the sultan about what action to take in Dhofar, another opposition front opened. During 1969 a group of Omani exiles in Iraq formed the National Democratic Front for the Liberation of Oman and the Arabian Gulf (NDFLOAG). In June 1970 a small party of NDFLOAG attacked the SAF base at Izki, near Nizwa in interior Oman. Although SAF easily repulsed the attack, information supplied by captured rebels led to the discovery of Chinese-supplied arms depots in Matrah and Sur.

By the early summer of 1970, it was clear that Sultan

Sa'id ibn Taimur was the principal threat to the stability of Oman. The promises of an end to years of poverty presented by oil exports had not been realized. Furthermore, Sa'id's own distrust of his people and repressive policies only contributed to the frustration and dissatisfaction of his subjects. A new Oman required a new leader.

Sultan of Oman Wearing Uniform, c. 1974

After Sultan Sa'id went into exile in London, his only son Qaboos ibn Sa'id Al Sa'id became the new sultan. On July 26, 1970 Sultan Qaboos addressed his people for the first time on radio, announcing his accession and plans for the future.

6

Sultan Qaboos and the Renaissance

THE COUP OF 1970

On the sweltering day of July 23, 1970, Buraik ibn Hamud al-Ghafiri, son of the governor of Dhofar, led a group of soldiers into the royal palace in Salalah to overthrow Sultan Sa'id ibn Taimur al-Sa'id. Although surprised, Sa'id and his personal bodyguard managed to fend off his attackers. Buraik, wounded in the melee, withdrew, gathered more troops, and staged a second assault. Finally, Sultan Sa'id, who had suffered a self-inflicted gunshot wound to the foot, agreed to surrender but only to a British military officer. That accomplished, Sa'id received medical attention and boarded a plane for exile to London. Oman's new era had begun.

Well, Muscat, 1910

The new sultan was Sa'id's only son, Qaboos ibn Sa'id Al-Sa'id. Sultan Qaboos had been born in Salalah in November 1940 to Sa'id's Dhofari wife. He had spent all of his boyhood in Salalah, where he received private tutoring in the royal palace. In 1958 Qaboos went to England for further tutoring before entering the British military academy at Sandhurst. Upon graduation in 1962, military duty in Germany, a course on municipal administration in England, and a world tour, the crown prince returned to Salalah. In Salalah Qaboos lived under virtual house arrest imposed by his suspicious father. Despite Sa'id's attempts to isolate his son, Qaboos became increasingly concerned

Well, Muscat, 1940

Donkeys drew buckets of water from these wells. The buckets were made from animal skins.

When Sultan Qaboos ibn Sa'id came to power in 1970, Oman lagged centuries behind the modern world. There were only three schools in the entire country—in Muscat, Matrah, and Salalah—no newspapers, radio or television, no civil service, and only one hospital with 23 beds. Muscat still closed its gates at night—and there were two graded but unpaved roads in the country. The average life expectancy of Omanis in 1970 was just 47 years. It has since risen to 68 years.

about conditions in Oman and began expressing those concerns to those few trusted individuals in the palace who were permitted to visit him. However, by 1970 conditions in Muscat and Oman had become so critical that even some of Sa'id ibn Taimur's advisers supported a change in the government.

News of the coup remained a secret for three days, but on July 26 Sultan Qaboos addressed his people for the first time on radio, announcing his accession and plans for the future. Several days later he proceeded to the capital, Muscat, a city that he had never visited. He also announced a new name for the country, now to be called only the Sultanate of Oman, symbolizing the end of the old division between Muscat and the interior. Unity required much more than a mere name change, though. Sultan Qaboos faced a number of problems and immediately set out to end the international isolation of his country, establish a modern governmental structure, and, most importantly, deal with the major threat to his government, the war in Dhofar.

FOREIGN POLICY

In 1970 Oman maintained diplomatic relations with only two countries: the United Kingdom and India. The sultanate was otherwise completely isolated from the rest of the world. The new sultan immediately began an effort to gain international recognition. Relations with neighboring Arab states were particularly critical, as the sultanate had border disputes with Saudi Arabia, the United Arab Emirates, and Iran, and support for both the exiled imam and the Dhofari insurgents came from them.

An "Omani Friendship Commission" visited Saudi Arabia in January 1971, paving the way for Sultan Qaboos's personal visit and meeting with King Faisal in December. It was a successful encounter because the two monarchs reached agreement on the imamate issue and began discussions to resolve their border disputes. Saudi Arabia also pledged aid to assist in Oman's economic development. A similar reconciliation occurred with the Emirates. Sheikh Zayid of Abu Dhabi—who would become president of the United Arab Emirates in 1971—was the first foreign head of state to visit Qaboos. He also promised financial aid and a willingness to resolve border issues. An early success in the new relationship came in 1974 when Saudi Arabia renounced all claims to the Buraimi Oasis, and Oman and Abu Dhabi reached agreement on the division of the region's nine villages. Lesser contacts with other Arab states brought some results, and although Iraq and South Yemen remained hostile, Oman gained recognition to the Arab League in 1971 and full diplomatic relations with nearly all Arab states by the end of 1972.

Iran was particularly important to the new sultan. Oman and Iran have long-standing close ties and share control of the strategically important Straits of Hormuz. Furthermore, Iran was the most powerful state in the region, and Shah Muhammad Reza Pahlevi shared Sultan Qaboos's concern for communist threats from the Soviet Union. Not surprisingly, Sultan Qaboos's first official foreign visit was to attend the October 1971 celebration of the 2,500th anniversary of the Persian monarchy. Oman and Iran quickly concluded border and security arrangements, and Iran became the major regional supporter of Oman in the war in Dhofar.

Sultan Qaboos also sought to expand Omani relations with the other major powers in the world. Sayyid Tariq ibn Taimur, the sultan's uncle and first prime minister, led efforts to gain European recognition. The dominant position of Great Britain in foreign affairs remained strong, especially as the United Kingdom continued to be the main trading partner and supplier of defense advice and aid.

France and the Netherlands extended recognition in 1972, to be followed by Spain and Germany. Sultan Qaboos did not seek relations with the Soviet Union and the People's Republic of China, active supporters of the rebels in Dhofar.

The United States recognized the Qaboos regime in 1972. Despite Oman's strategic importance, the United States maintained a low-level presence, seeing the sultanate as part of the British sphere of influence. However, in 1975 the relationship between the two countries became much stronger when Sultan Qaboos granted the United States military access privileges to the airbase at Masirah Island. The United States also began providing military assistance.

CREATION OF A GOVERNMENT

Sultan Qaboos's second order of business was to establish a modern government. Sultan Sa'id had depended on a small number of family members to provide the very basics of government, and these officials were then mostly ignored. A major problem facing the new sultan was the fact that he hardly knew anyone since he had been so isolated in Salalah. Sa'id's advisers, especially the defense secretary Hugh Oldman, proved very willing to assist. They set up an advisery council to guide Qaboos. Their first act—probably done without the agreement of the Sultan—was to invite Sayyid Tariq ibn Taimur to return from exile in Germany to serve as prime minister and begin the task of setting up new ministries and hiring new officials. A power struggle between sultan and prime minister resulted.

Sayyid Tariq, Sultan Sa'id's brother, had been born in 1922 and was a cosmopolitan man who had been educated in Turkey, Germany, and India. Sultan Sa'id had appointed him to various government posts, including a short time in the army, then as head of the Muscat municipality, and finally as the governor of Oman following the reunification

Minaret at the Sultan's Palace, c. 1997-1998

On his return from living abroad in 1962 Sultan Qaboos had been kept in virtual isolation in the palace in Salalah. When he became the sultan of Oman in 1970 he went to the capital, Muscat, a city he had never visited.

of the country in 1957. However, Sa'id dismissed Tariq in 1960, and he went into exile later in the year, eventually settling in Germany. Tariq had a reputation for being a "liberal" and supporting a constitutional monarchy. Qaboos thought that Tariq also wanted to be the sultan. The relationship between nephew and uncle was cool, and a power struggle resulted.

Although Tariq was often busy with foreign affairs and settling personal matters in Germany, he moved quickly to

designed to address the grievances of the Dhofari population against the sultanate and a more aggressive military policy aimed at defeating the hard-core rebels.

The first step in the hearts-and-minds campaign was the announcement of a general pardon for all rebels who surrendered to the government. The amnesty produced the desired effect, with hundreds of tribespeople, whose opposition to the government was personal rather than ideological, defecting to the government.

The second step came in 1971 with the organization of the *firqat*—Dhofari paramilitary units—an idea inspired by Salim ibn Mubarak, the former second in command of the liberation movement and one of the first Dhofaris to accept Qaboos's amnesty. The firqat were 100-man units formed of the rebels who had surrendered to the government and were then armed and trained by British Special Air Service advisers to fight against their erstwhile allies. The firqat were not particularly effective fighters, but they were an important symbol of the sultan's trust and desire to help the people of Dhofar because they provided a prestigious means of employment and financial stability.

Finally, the government organized Civil Action Teams. These teams were flown into areas secured by government forces to provide immediate medical care to the population. They would dig a well, set up a mosque, a clinic, a school, and a store, and then build a road (and later an airstrip) to establish communication links with neighboring areas.

On the military side, Qaboos insured that his armed forces had the manpower, supplies, and expertise to win the war. The Sultan's Armed Forces (SAF) was expanded with the formation of a new 10,000-man Dhofar Brigade. Transportation capabilities also increased with the purchase of eight helicopters and eight air transport planes. Finally, Qaboos invited the British to send military advisers from the Special Air Services unit to train his army.

Man at Well in Oman, c. 1980-1997
A man stands at a well in Taqah in Dhofar, Oman.

Despite these efforts the forces of the Popular Front for the Liberation of the Occupied Arabian Gulf (PFLOAG) remained on the offensive, retaking several positions captured during late 1970 and early 1971 and securing complete control of the strategic road between Salalah and Thumrait. By the fall of 1971, SAF was prepared to launch an offensive. Strategy focused on the establishment of permanent bases in the mountains. Although the bases would be of minimal strategic importance, they were seen as having great symbolic importance. Accordingly, Operation Jaguar in October 1971 succeeded in capturing the town of Madina al-Haqq, although it was abandoned during the monsoon. This was followed in April 1972 with Operation Simba, which captured the town of Sarfait, close to the South Yemeni border, and managed to hold it through the fall and winter.

PFLOAG responded with a vicious offensive. This began with a reorganization of PFLOAG under Muhammad ibn Ahmad al-Ghassani and a purge of those who were generally Dhofari nationalists as opposed to hard-line Marxists. Then came the military assault. In June 1972 a rocket attack on the Salalah airbase wounded 12 British soldiers. One month later PFLOAG attacks on Mirbat and Taqa nearly succeeded in overrunning these towns. Finally, in November the PFLOAG sought once again to take the struggle to northern Oman with an uprising in Matrah. Fortunately, security forces received advanced notice, and a raid on their base in Matrah resulted in the capture of 90 rebels and their weapons cache. Just as in 1970, an attack on northern Oman failed.

Unlike 1970, however, the new government was now in position to take the offensive. SAF strategy focused on clearing rebels from Dhofar's eastern (Jabal Samhan) and central (Jabal Qara) regions, where they were weakest and isolating the remainder in the western (Jabal Qamar) region. The latter was accomplished by the construction of a series of defensive lines to cut rebel movement across Dhofar. Omani efforts were also assisted by the arrival of Iranian and Jordanian military personnel.

The PFLOAG again reorganized, again limiting its horizons, at its July 1974 conference in Aden. The broader goals of revolution throughout the region were abandoned and the group became the Popular Front for the Liberation of Oman (PFLO). Despite the surface changes, the organization stood on its last leg. In December 1975 Iranian forces and the SAF began the final stage of the war with a major military campaign along the Omani-South Yemen border. In January 1975 the rebel "capital" at Rakhyut fell to government forces.

Attention then turned to the Shershitti cave complex, the last stronghold of the PFLO. There, regular-army soldiers from South Yemen joined the 1,800 PFLO rebels. The PFLO also began to use surface-to-air missiles and received additional artillery support from across the Yemeni border. The PFLO offered stiff resistance; however, in October government forces captured Shershitti. South Yemen forces withdrew across the border. Finally, in December the SAF captured the last rebel stronghold at Dhalqut. On December 11, 1975, Sultan Qaboos announced victory in the war in Dhofar.

Sporadic military action continued into 1976, and South Yemeni forces occasionally fired a shell across the border, but by the end of 1976, Sultan Qaboos had effectively consolidated his hold on the administration in Oman and eliminated the major threat to the security of his country. The sultan could now turn his attention to the further political and economic development of his state.

Mideast Oman, 2001

An Omani man enters the Sultan Qaboos Grand Mosque to attend prayers. The mosque is in Muscat, the capital of Oman.

7

The New Oman

*I*t is popular in Oman to describe the reign of Sultan Qaboos ibn Sa'id Al-Sa'id as a renaissance, a rebirth. In many ways the characterization is true. With the defeat of the rebels in Dhofar and the income made available by oil exports, Qaboos had unified his country and possessed the means to provide basic public services, including security, education, health care, communications, transportation, and a role in the world for all of the people of Oman. Under the able leadership of Sultan Qaboos, Oman has made great progress toward becoming a modern state.

Muscat House Outside the City Wall, 1940

The houses located outside the Muscat city wall were constructed of such materials as mud, wood, palm branches, and corrugated iron sheets.

In the late 1970s and early 1980s, Muscat began construction of major housing projects, which have eliminated the type of dwelling pictured above.

CONSULTATION AND BASIC LAW

By 1976 the basic structure of Omani administration had taken shape. Periodically since that time, cabinets have been shuffled, ministries established, abolished, or reorganized, but there has been a high degree of continuity in leadership personnel. Some of Qaboos's early advisers and ministers have left the cabinet, either through death (Qais ibn Abd al-Munim al-Zawawi in 1995 and Sayyid Fahr ibn Taimur Al-Sa'id in 1996) or through retirement (Muhammad ibn Zubair and Said Ahmad al-Shanfari), but stability has been provided through such men as Sayyid Fahd ibn Mahmud Al-Sa'id, Sayyid Faisal ibn Ali Al-Sa'id, Sayyid Thuwaini ibn Shihab Al-Sa'id, Abd al-Aziz ibn Muhammad Ruwas, Sayyid Badr ibn Sa'ud Al Bu Sa'id, Hamud ibn Abdullah al-Harithi, and many others. These veterans are being balanced by a new generation of "technocrats"—ministers with significant training and experience in their areas of responsibility.

While stable ministerial government has provided an able administration, by far the greatest development in Oman has been the evolution of consultative government. Unlike most of his predecessors but very much in keeping with Oman's Ibadi political tradition, Sultan Qaboos has made some effort at seeking the opinion of his subjects. This process began in 1975 when he initiated an annual "meet the people" tour, a two-week event designed to allow the sultan to hear directly the concerns of Omanis. These tours continue to this day.

An institutional basis for public consultation came with the formation of the Majlis al-Istishari Li al-Dawla (State Consultative Council, or SCC). The SCC held its first meetings in November 1981 with 44 members, divided among representatives of the government, business, and geographic regions. A nomination procedure provided a list of candidates from whom the sultan appointed members. The council met three times a year and was empowered to make recommendations to the government on economic and social matters.

In 1991 a more representative Majlis al-Shura (Consultative Council) replaced the SCC. Unlike the SCC, Majlis membership came only from geographic regions, with each of Oman's 59 *wilayats* (districts) nominating candidates.

Also unlike the SCC, the Majlis selection process involved public nomination, with all males of at least 30 years of age and of "high esteem [and] good reputation" eligible to participate. The sultan still appointed Majlis members. Majlis duties remained advisery on matters related to economic and social development.

Important changes occurred in both membership and the selection process of the Majlis. By far the most significant change came with the inclusion of women both as nominators and as candidates for office. As a result, two women—Shukur bint Muhammad al-Ghamari from Muscat and Tayyiba bint Muhammad al-Ma'awali from Sib—were nominated and appointed to the Majlis in 1994. Majlis membership has also increased, with a proportional representation system granting larger districts two representatives. Finally, although the sultan continues to approve the nomination list, the Majlis has become an elected body.

A second consultative body came into existence in 1997 with the creation of the Majlis al-Dawla (Council of State). This "upper House" is completely appointed, and membership is based on "nobility" as defined by one's service to Oman. Its original 42 members included three women.

The Majlis al-Dawla came into existence by virtue of the proclamation in November 1996 of the "Basic Statute of the State." This constitutionlike document defines how the Omani state functions and includes chapters on succession, the responsibilities of the head of state, consultative structures, the judiciary, and public rights and duties.

The major development since the proclamation of the basic law came in June 2001 with the reorganization of the judiciary system. The legal reform created a formal court structure, including an appellate and a supreme court, to deal with civil, commercial, penal, and personal law. The new court system represents an important guarantee of judicial independence and human rights promised in the Basic Statue.

Although these significant political developments have the support of the overwhelming majority of the Omani people, a recurring problem has been the extent to which high-level government employees have utilized their official positions to profit personally. Although "conflict of interest" regulations have been in place since the early 1970s, concern about too close a relationship between politics and business did lead some high government officials—like Muhammad ibn Zubair al-Hutti—to resign from the government. Others did not demonstrate such high levels of integrity. Dissatisfaction reached a peak in 1994 when 194 people were arrested for sedition and accused of attempting to overthrow the government. Although these people were labeled "Muslim fundamentalists," their concerns seem to have been more with government corruption than religious issues. Significant steps were taken to address this matter in 2001 with the arrest, trial, and conviction of a number of former government officials, most notably a long-time finance officer, Muhammad ibn Musa al-Yusuf, for graft.

ECONOMIC DEVELOPMENT

The Omani renaissance has been fueled by oil, for without the continuing income derived from petroleum exports, Sultan Qaboos would not have possessed the resources necessary for development. Despite efforts to diversify, petroleum still provides 90 percent of Omani state revenues and promises to remain the dominant sector of the economy.

Development of petroleum resources has been a partnership between the government and Petroleum Development Oman (PDO), which is only 60 percent government owned. Since the late 1970s, PDO has followed a policy of aggressive oil-field development and enhanced-recovery techniques (technologies that force more oil from wells than natural flow) that have steadily increased production from about 300 barrels per day in 1980 to about 1,000,000 barrels per day in 2001. The government has also encouraged other oil companies to contribute to the country's petroleum development through the awarding of exploration and production concessions in areas not controlled by PDO.

While oil exports provide the greatest share of government revenues, Oman has moved toward secondary petroleum based industries to help diversify the economy. In 1982 the Oman Refinery Company began operation to provide automotive gasoline to the local market. More recent development focuses on natural gas. Formerly a by-product of oil production, gas was for many years "flared off" (burned) as waste. In 1978 PDO began collecting and processing natural gas for power generation and as a fuel for cooking. In the early 1990s the government examined the possibility of exporting surplus natural gas production. Construction of the Oman Liquid Natural Gas Company complex near Sur began in 1994, with the first exports coming in 2000.

Oman's second most important mineral resource was copper. This mineral traces its history in Oman back to ancient days when mines inland from Sohar supplied the western Indian Ocean basin. A Canadian company began exploration in 1973 and discovered 60 possible sites. The Oman Mining Company began operations in 1983, and production peaked at 15,000 tons of copper in 1989. However, these resources are now almost depleted, and Oman imports copper ore for processing.

In addition to mineral resources, Oman economic planners have also directed attention to traditional agriculture and fisheries resources, activities that continue to employ a very high percentage of the Omani population. Oman has limited agricultural lands due to a lack of water, but the distinctive

Oil Drilling Macine in Oil Field, c. 1980-1997

While oil exports provide the greatest share of government revenues, Oman has moved into secondary petroleum-based industries, such as providing gasoline to the local market.

irrigation system based on manmade underground channels, known as *falaj,* that help to collect and distribute meager water resources, do make farming possible. Traditional products such as dates and frankincense provide the basis for food-related industries.

While hopes for agricultural self-sufficiency are doubtful, fisheries resources are much more promising. Oman's coastal waters offer many commercial species of fish and crustaceans. Government-financed programs to develop small-scale fisheries—by providing boats and processing and marketing facilities—supply the local market. Larger-scale commercial fisheries, such as the government-owned Oman National Fisheries Company, have made Oman the largest exporter of fish and fish products in the region. One negative consequence has been overfishing.

Omani economic planners hoped that industrialization would also establish another alternative to the petroleum-based economy. The government provided incentives for industrialization through low-interest loans and the creation of industrial parks that provided basic infrastructure. Early industries included small-scale enterprises producing materials (ceramic tile, aluminum door- and window frames, plastic pipe) to supply the building boom of the late 1970s. During the mid-1980s the focus shifted to import replacement activities, with local companies producing goods such as automotive parts, air conditioners, and a variety of food products. By the early 1990s the focus had again shifted to the production of export products, most notably ready-made clothing. These efforts witnessed very modest successes—especially as less than 20 percent of those employed in the industrial sector were Omani, the rest being expatriate labor, mostly from South Asia.

Oman's economic future would appear to be firmly tied to the petroleum sector, with oil and natural gas exports continuing to provide the bulk of state revenues. Fisheries will also be important, although much better controls to prevent overfishing are necessary. Insufficient water resources will limit agriculture; a lack of natural resources, small market, and human resources will limit industrialization.

SOCIAL DEVELOPMENT

When Qaboos became Sultan in July 1970, Oman lacked both the infrastructure and programs for social development. Sultan Sa'id's advisers had prepared a few plans for roads, a port, a new airport, electricity, and water, but nothing had been implemented. Efforts during the years of the Dhofar war focused on these endeavors. As a result, Port Qaboos in Matrah, the Sib International Airport, the highways linking Muscat to Sohar, Nizwa, Rustaq, and Sur, television and radio stations, and the Ghubrah water desalinization and power plant were all completed. Since 1976 these have been expanded to include a second port and airport in Salalah, a national highway system that links all major towns with paved highways—including the Nizwa-Thumrait road providing the first road link between northern Oman and Dhofar—and national telephone and electric grids.

Infrastructure development did not occur at the expense of the environment, and Sultan Qaboos has received international recognition for his conservation activities. Oman's first environmental law dates to 1974, and laws in 1979 established national parks and nature preserves. The most important conservation project in Oman involved the reintroduction into the wild of the nearly extinct Arabian Oryx, a long-horned antelope believed to be the origin of the myth of the unicorn. In 1984 Oman became the first state in the region to establish a Ministry of Environmental Affairs. Most recent environmental programs have focused on marine ecology and pollution control.

The new regime also placed great emphasis on educational development. In 1970 the government ran only three schools for boys. The Ministry of Education was one of the first on the new ministries established in 1970. Early efforts focused on elementary education for both boys and girls, with advanced students being sent abroad on government scholarships. A World Bank review team criticized these efforts, and in 1975 the ministry launched a major reform of the system, with greater attention paid to middle and secondary school development.

Oman now boasts a comprehensive education system. Elementary schools emphasize the study of Arabic and English languages, math, science, social studies, and Islamic studies. In junior high school students choose either an academic or technical track. High-school placement is competitive, and students choose academic tracks related to science, Islamic studies, or arts and literature or vocational tracks in teacher education, business, technology, or agriculture. Girls receive the same academic training, but a "domestic education" component, including nutrition and child care, is also added.

Sultan Qaboos University, Oman's first institution of higher education, opened in September 1986 with 580 students. It is a comprehensive university, with colleges of education and Islamic sciences, engineering, sciences, agriculture, medicine, arts, and commerce and economics. Post-secondary vocational education also expanded with the opening of the Oman Technical Industrial College and four teacher-training colleges, all in 1984. The number of teacher colleges has since expanded to eight. Private colleges began operating in the sultanate in 1995.

Preservation and promotion of Oman's rich cultural heritage was an important part of government support for education. These activities fell under the direction of the Ministry of National Heritage and Culture, administered by Sayyid Faisal ibn Ali Al-Sa'id, a cousin of the Sultan and a former schoolteacher. The ministry holds primary responsibility for the restoration and operation of Oman's historical monuments, most notably its many forts and palaces, such as the great palace at Jabrin. In addition, the ministry operates the national museum, the national library and archive, and provides support for traditional handicrafts.

The Omani government also devoted considerable time and resources to health care. During the 1970s Oman received assistant from the World Health Organization and

Jabrin Palace, 1998

The Ministry of National Heritage and Culture now holds responsibility for the restoration and operation of Oman's many historical monuments, including the 17th-century fortress, Jabin Palace.

UNICEF to attack the country's two most serious diseases: the eye disease trachoma and malaria. By 2000 both diseases had been nearly eliminated. This success is attributable to the National Health Program that promotes preventive health care through immunization and education programs in all areas of health care.

A network of comprehensive hospitals, primary-care

clinics and mobile health units provides health care to all parts of the country. Like most developing countries, Oman does suffer a shortage of health-care professionals, but such facilities as the Institute of Health Science provides training for nurses, paramedical staff, and pharmacists, and the medical school at Sultan Qaboos University trains about 40 new doctors per year.

Omani social development has been characterized by its inclusiveness. From their beginnings, both education and health care emphasized the central role of women in society. Women play a public role in the work force, in business, and in politics.

OMAN AND THE WORLD

As the earlier chapters in this book demonstrate, Oman has a long tradition of interaction with the rest of the world. During the 19th century, Muscat was an international city, hosting merchants from India, Iran, Africa, Europe, the Americas, and the rest of the Arab world. World War I and the isolationism of the reign of Sa'id ibn Taimur served to limit Oman's contacts to Britain and its immediate neighbors. Since 1970, though, Oman has reassumed its active role in the world. Relations with near neighbors have been most important, and Oman has become an important regional actor through its participation in the Gulf Cooperation Council. In the wider world, focus has been devoted to another historical regional connection, the Indian Ocean, and Oman has been a leader in the formation of the Indian Ocean Rim Association for Regional Cooperation. However, Oman's relations with the great powers of the world have also been very important.

With the conclusion of the Dhofar war, Sultan Qaboos turned his attention to more active cooperation among the Persian Gulf states. Talks focusing on some kind of Gulf strategic cooperation began in 1976. However, the outbreak of the Iran-Iraq war in 1980 prompted immediate action, and in February 1981 Oman, the United Arab Emirates, Qatar, Kuwait, Bahrain, and Saudi Arabia joined to create the Gulf Cooperation Council (GCC). GCC initiatives have focused on the integration of defense and economic policies. Oman plays an active role in all discussions, although it has generally favored an evolutionary process, fearing that too-rapid development of a joint defense pact might be seen as threatening to neighbor Iran and that full economic integration would benefit the richer, more fully developed northern members. Outside of the GCC, Oman strengthened ties with all of its contiguous neighbors and has settled all border disputes.

Oman also became more active in wider Middle Eastern affairs. Sultan Qaboos's policies toward the Arab-Israeli dispute best demonstrate his independent foreign policy. Although Oman supports the right of Palestinian self-determination, the return of East Jerusalem to Arab rule, and the Arab League's economic boycott of Israel, Sultan Qaboos believed that successful resolution of the conflict could only come through dialogue among all parties. Accordingly, Oman, along with Somalia and Sudan, broke with Arab ranks to support Anwar Sadat's peace initiative with Israel in 1979. Similarly, Oman backed Jordanian initiatives for a negotiated settlement in the 1980s. When the Madrid Conference and the Oslo Accords of 1993 promised a major thaw in Arab-Israeli relations, Oman invited Israel to participate in a regional water conference and began trade talks. Unfortunately, the outbreak of the al-Aqsa Intifada in 2001 resulted in an end to that cooperation because Oman denounced Israeli intransigence.

Oman also continued to maintain a close relationship with western allies Great Britain and the United States. Great Britain remains Oman's closest ally, although the

number of British political and military advisers diminished considerably during the past decade. The relationship
with the United States grew after 1977 when Sultan Qaboos
granted American access to Omani military facilities.
Oman then became a recipient of American military assistance, and the United States Army Corps of Engineers
began upgrading Omani facilities. Oman provided valuable
assistance during the 1991 Gulf War and during the 2002
war in Afghanistan.

Economic considerations play a major role in determin-
ing policy with the rest of the world. Especially important in
this regard is Oman's relations with Indian Ocean neighbors
Pakistan, India, and East Africa. Oman has a long history
of commercial relationships in this region, and South Asia
continues to provide considerable human resources in both
skilled and unskilled labor. Accordingly, Oman became a
charter member of the Indian Ocean Rim Association for
Regional Cooperation in 1997.

Sultan Qaboos's 30 years in power serves as an excellent
example of the two themes that have dominated Omani
history for the past 250 years: the desire for a righteous
leader within the Ibadi religious tradition and the country's
active role in world affairs. Beginning with the election of
Ahmad ibn Sa'id as imam in 1753 through the beginning of
the 20th century, a member of the Al Bu Sa'id family either
served as imam or challenged a relative for the position.
While a dynamic leader like Sa'id ibn Sultan could rule
Oman without being imam, the desire for the religious ideal
dominated political events. During the 20th century,
Omanis turned to leaders outside the Al Bu Sa'id. Although
Muscat continued under Al Bu Sa'id rule, an elected imam
ruled in Oman. The division between Muscat and Oman
continued until the 1950s, when Sultan Sa'id ibn Taimur
and his British allies drove the imam into exile. However,
full Omani unity only emerged under Sultan Qaboos ibn

Sa'id who overthrew his father in 1970 and began wide-ranging social and economic development programs and political reforms that reintroduced Ibadi principles of consultation and righteousness. Although not elected imam, Sultan Qaboos did fulfill the goal of "decreeing what is lawful and prohibiting what is unlawful."

Under Qaboos, Oman also saw its traditional role in world affairs reestablished. Oman's important in world affairs dates to ancient times, when caravans carrying frankincense set out from places like Ubar to the rest of the world. During the first centuries of Al Bu Sa'id rule, especially during the reign of Sa'id ibn Sultan, the port of Muscat became a global city. Merchants from around the world settled in the port and brought an abundance of trade to the country. During the troubled times of the early 20th century, the trade diminished, and Oman became isolated for the first time in its long history. That isolation ended under Sultan Qaboos, and Oman again became an active member of the world community. However, rather than frankincense or other agriculture products, Omani oil now finds its way to the markets of China, Europe, and the Americas.

Gallery of Photographs
from Oman

Dhofar

Dhofar is an historical region in southern Oman and makes up about one-third of the nation's total area. It is Oman's most fertile region and the world's leading source of frankincense.

Dhofar is one of the locations suggested by historians for the Biblical area of Ophir—an unidentified region mentioned in the Old Testament that was famous for its gold. The town of Salalah, on the coast of the Arabian Sea, was described by Marco Polo in the late 13th century as being prosperous because of the abundance of frankincense trees.

Dhofari, 1930

Dhofari Villagers, 1930

Qara' from Dhofar, 1930

In 1984, the British explorer Theodore Bent (1852-97) became the first Westerner to encounter the Qara' people.

The rugged Qara' Mountains in Dhofar rise to heights of over 4,000 feet. Bent described the picturesque valleys, lakes, and waterfalls, and " the interesting and peculiar occupants of the hills, the Garas (Qara') who speak a language of their own.

Jebali Tribesmen, 1934

The Jebalis are a subgroup of the Qara' tribe, who live in the mountainous areas and raise cattle.

Omanis, Sib, 1903

Sib was the first major settlement north of Muscat. A fairly unremarkable town, Sib remained a small market area for local fishermen and farmers. There was a busy *souq* (market) that attracted people from the surrounding region.

Today, 100 years later, this area is dominated by Sib International Airport. The airport is about ten miles from the town. Twenty-two miles from Muscat, it is the official gateway to Oman. The International and Domestic Terminals include facilities such as a 24-hour bank, a 24-hour cafeteria and restaurant, a hotel, and a new duty-free complex.

Fishing, Muscat, 1905

This *houris,* or seagoing canoe is hollowed out of a single tree. It is still used by fishermen today. A traveler of centuries ago noted that Omani fishermen looked strange using paddles "as diggers do their spades in the earth, not rowing in the Grecian manner with oars."

Fishing is important to Oman. Through the centuries droughts caused crop failures in the interior. But dried fish brought inland from the coast supplemented the diet of people whose eyes never saw the sea. There are dozens of different varieties of fish, but certain types of shark are more commonly eaten, together with kingfish, marlin, tuna and sardines.

Harasis Women, 1908

The nomadic Harasis live in the Oman interior near the Yemen border.

This photograph was taken by an American missionary living in the Persian Gulf area. He described the Harasis as having "dwellings constructed of boulders or rocks and they subsist on their flocks." The women wore "heavy silver anklets, ear-rings, bracelets, and nose jewels . . . also the peculiar veil worn over the face." He found these people "wonderful in their hospitality" and "eager for medical help."

Al Wahibah, Nomad, 1925

The al Wahibah nomads live in the al Wahibah desert in east-central Oman. It is estimated that this large tribe consisted of about 30,000 people in the 1920s. They were noted for having the swiftest breed of camels in the region. To Omanis, camels are beautiful. They derive as great a pleasure from looking at a good camel, as others get from looking at a good horse. Indeed, there is a tremendous feeling of power, rhythm, and grace about these great animals.

The al Wahibah desert consists of honey-colored sand dunes that are dark red at their base and rise to heights of more than 200 feet. There is very little surface water. Underground water is reached by tunneling into the earth at a shallow angle until the water table is reached.

In 1985-87, the Oman Wahibah Sands Project was organized by the Royal Geographic Society and the Omani government. The purpose of the project was to study the geomorphology—the study of land forms and their origin—of the sand dunes and the interaction of organisms within this environment. Also, the project attempted to assess the impact of changes in the desert on its nomadic inhabitants.

Allen, Calvin H. Jr. *Oman: Modernization of the Sultanate*. Boulder, Colo.: Westview, 1987.

Allen, Calvin H. Jr., and Lynn Rigsbee. *Oman under Qaboos*. London: Frank Cass, 2000.

Anthony, John Duke. *Historical and Cultural Dictionary of the Sultanate of Oman and the Emirates of Eastern Arabia*. Metuchen, N.J.: Scarecrow Press, 1976.

Clapp, Nicholas. *The Road to Ubar*. Boston: Houghton Mifflin, 1998.

Eickelman, Christine. *Women & Community in Oman*. New York: New York University Press, 1984.

Hawley, Donald. *Oman and Its Renaissance*. London: Stacey International, 1990.

Peterson, J. E. *Oman in the Twentieth Century*. London: Croom Helm, 1978.

Phillips, Wendell. *Oman: A History*. London: Reynal & Company, 1967.

———. *Unknown Oman*. New York: David McKay, 1966.

Skeet, Ian. *Masqat and Oman: End of an Era*. London: Faber & Faber, 1974.

———. *Oman: Politics & Development*. London: Macmillan, 1992.

BOOKS:

Allen, Calvin H. Jr. *Oman: Modernization of the Sultanate*. Boulder, Colo.: Westview, 1987.

Allen, Calvin H. Jr. and Lynn Rigsbee. *Oman under Qaboos*. London: Frank Cass, 2000.

Anthony, John Duke. *Historical and Cultural Dictionary of the Sultanate of Oman and the Emirates of Eastern Arabia*. Metuchen, N.J.: Scarecrow Press, 1976.

Badger, George. *History of the imams and Seyyids of Oman*. New York: Burt Franklin, c. 1963, reprint of 1871 original.

Eickelman, Christine. *Women & Community in Oman*. New York: New York University Press, 1984.

Kechichian, Joseph. *Oman and the World*, Santa Monica, Calif.: Rand, 1995.

Landen, Robert. *Oman Since 1856*. Princeton, N.J.: Princeton University Press, 1967.

Maurizi, Vincenzo. *History of Seyd Said*. Cambridge: Oleander Press, 1984.

Peterson, J. E. *Oman in the Twentieth Century*. London: Croom Helm, 1978.

Risso, Patricia. *Oman & Masqat: An Early Modern History*. New York: St. Martin's Press, 1986.

Thesiger, Wilfred. *Arabian Sands*. New York: E. P. Dutton & Company, 1959.

Wilkinson, John. *The imamate Tradition of Oman*. Cambridge: Cambridge University Press, 1987.

WEB SITE SOURCES:

www.arab.net/oman/oman_contents.html

gulf2000.Columbia.edu/country/oman

www.oman.org

www.omaninfo.com

www.omanet.com

www.omanews.com

www.omantimes.com

www.omanobserver.com

Cover: Royal Geographic Society
Frontispiece: Royal Geographic Society

page:
58: Hulton/Archive by Getty Images
74: Hulton/Archive by Getty Images
87: Wolfgang Kaehler/Corbis
80: Bettmann/Corbis

91: K.M. Westermann/Corbis
94: AP/Wide World Photos
101: Eye Ubiquitous/Corbis
105: David G. Houser/Corbis

Unless otherwise credited all photographs in this book © Royal Geographic Society.
No reproduction of images without permission.
Royal Geographic Society
1 Kensington Gore
London SW7 2AR

Unless otherwise credited the photographs in this book are from the Royal Geographic Society Picture Library. Most are being published for the first time.

The Royal Geographic Society Picture Library provides an unrivaled source of over half a million images of the peoples and landscapes from around the globe. Photographs date from the 1840s onwards on a variety of subjects including the British Colonial Empire, deserts, exploration, indigenous peoples, landscapes, remote destinations, and travel.

Photography, beginning with the daguerreotype in 1839, is only marginally younger than the Society, which encouraged its explorers to use the new medium from its earliest days. From the remarkable mid-19th century black-and-white photographs to color transparencies of the late 20th century, the focus of the collection is not the generic stock shot but the portrayal of man's resilience, adaptability and mobility in remote parts of the world.

In organizing this project, we have incurred many debts of gratitude. Our first, though, is to the professional staff of the Picture Library for their generous assistance, especially to Joanna Wright, Picture Library Manager.

CALVIN H. ALLEN JR. is professor of Middle Eastern history at the University of Memphis. He has a Ph.D. in history and an M.A. in Near Eastern Languages and Literature from the University of Washington and a B.A. in Political Science from the University of Pittsburgh. Allen is the author of *Oman: Modernization of the Sultanate* (Westview, 1987) and, with Lynn Rigsbee, *Oman under Qaboos* (Frank Cass, 2000), as well as a number of articles on Oman.

AKBAR S. AHMED holds the Ibn Khaldun Chair of Islamic Studies at the School of International Service of American University. He is actively involved in the study of global Islam and its impact on contemporary society. He is the author of many books on contemporary Islam, including *Discovering Islam: Making Sense of Muslim History and Society,* which was the basis for a six-part television program produced by the BBC called *Living Islam.* Ahmed has been visiting professor and the Stewart Fellow in the Humanities at Princeton University, as well as visiting professor at Harvard University and Cambridge University.